Rapid Prototyping
For Object-Oriented Systems

Mark Mullin

Addison-Wesley Publishing Company, Inc.

Reading, Massachusetts Menlo Park, California New York
Don Mills, Ontario Wokingham, England Amsterdam Bonn Sydney
Singapore Tokyo Madrid San Juan

Many of the designations used by manufacturers and sellers to distinguish their products are claimed as trademarks. Where those designations appear in this book and Addison-Wesley was aware of a trademark claim, the designations have been printed in initial capital letters.

Library of Congress Cataloging-in-Publication Data
Mullin, Mark.
    Rapid prototyping for object-oriented systems/Mark Mullin.
p.   cm.
Includes index.
ISBN 0-201-55024-5
    1. Computer software--Development. 2. Object-oriented programming
(Computer Science) I. Title.
QA76.76.D47M84 1990
005.1--dc20   90-39645

Production Editor: Amorette Pedersen
Set in 11-point Palatino by Benchmark Productions

ABCDEFGHIJ-MW-943210
First Printing, July 1990

For Leonard R. Minster, who made my rather bizarre education possible.

For Hilary and Tom, for a fateful introduction, so long ago.

For my clients, especially one group I've never been able to properly thank.

For Arthur and Leinie, for many things.

Acknowledgments

My special thanks go to Donna Holliday and Jim Lloyd, who rescued me from the D.C. contracting wars. Definitely a sword to plowshare operation. Also to the management and staff of Softview, Inc. who have created one of the most pleasant working environments I have encountered.

Thanks to Dennis Post and Mike, who provided the initial vehicle for my explorations of OOP. My special thanks go to Mike, for it was the two of us who evolved a concept of rapid prototyping before we knew there was such a creature. And to our benefactor, who took abuse but little credit.

Again, thanks to my father for being a steady sounding board on the literary aspects of the book, as well as for some invaluable Russian and Latin phrases. I also owe a debt of gratitude to my stepmother Leinie, for a little applied nagging at the appropriate times. If it weren't for the two of them, you might not be reading this.

Many thanks to software ninjas, Phil Taylor, Christine Hokans, and William Liebig. I wonder if another project could stand having us reassembled.

More thanks to Phil, especially for some fanciful brainstorming sessions that later became a reality. And to Chris, for a pleasant introduction to Hawaii.

Special thanks to my partners in crime, John Allen and Jerry "no known relation" Allen. Also to General Jeff and Jack Carpenter. Soon, gentlemen, soon.

I am indebted to Timothy C. Taylor for regular stress relief sessions. Party on dude! But can I wear a helmet the next time?

Thanks to the CAP burglars of the FTS-2000 project, especially Gerry Palmer. I only hope Jim Stahl has finally recovered from the onslaught. And I still call that stupid machine "Ralphie," in case anyone's interested.

Thanks to Symantec and especially Greg Dow.

Once again, my sincere thanks to my editor, Chris Williams, and the production editors, Amy Pedersen and Allison Cox of Benchmark Productions. You have been more than patient and I certainly appreciate it.

Finally, my thanks to all of you who have read *Object Oriented Program Design* and are preparing to read this book. I do realize that I deviate from the norm, as far as computer books go, and I'm grateful that you find this appropriate. I can only help that I've made some task of yours a little easier.

And once again to Apple Computer, for a useable machine. I guess now that I'm a developer, I can take some credit too.

Table of Contents

Introduction

Rapid Prototyping

This book deals with the concept of *rapid prototyping*, a process where specifications for a piece of software are developed by interaction between a *software developer*, a *client*, and a *prototype program*. Rapid prototyping is used when a client cannot initially define the requirements for a piece of software to a degree necessary to satisfy more traditional design methodologies, such as those defined by Edward Yourdon and Michael Jackson.

I would argue this is the way in which most software is developed. Although the previous methodologies are complete and rigid systems, they often fail in the field when they confront real software development tasks. The reason for this is simple. Formal design methodologies impose a heavy prerequisite on the development process because they require that the client or end user have a clear idea of exactly what they want and how it is to behave. Unfortunately, clients rarely have this complete a grasp on their problem; they usually assume their responsibilities are simpler, namely, they:

- Recognize that a problem exists
- Find an expert to solve the problem

For this reason, rapid prototyping, or *exploratory programming*, is an excellent mechanism to use for extracting hard specifications from the client so we can determine what they want. We are no longer confronted by the requirement that they initially define the exact nature of their problem and most of the required solution.

Rapid prototyping (RP) is not just a "feel good" process. It operates within a clearly defined paradigm, expects certain environmental constraints to be satisfied, and expects clients and developers to proceed from start to finish by way of a specific path. What is different about RP is that it doesn't require as much initial definition, but allows for the definition of the problem to be developed over time.

The Book

This book deals with the issues involved in a successful RP effort. It will take you from the initial client meeting to the point where the prototype has been completed and the final system is to be implemented. For examples, the specific language used in this book is Smalltalk, but this is not a general book on Smalltalk programming. Smalltalk provides you with a contextual example so you can see how a computer language can be used as a vehicle for rapid prototyping.

In flipping through this book, you may notice that it doesn't contain a great deal of code. This is true—I'm not a cookbook author. My intent is not to provide you with code to type into a computer; I will provide you with an understanding of how such code is crafted. You'll learn how rapid prototyping is done, how to design for reusability and portability, and how to extract specifications from a client.

While reading this book, keep a text on Smalltalk handy. (An excellent tutorial comes with the Digitalk Smalltalk/V package). You'll find Dan Shafer's book, *Practical Smalltalk* (Springer-Verlag), helpful.

The Author

This subject is far from academic to me; in fact, I have distrust of many things academic for the simple reason that they don't work so well in the real world. Structured programming, as taught in college, is wonderful, primarily because a professor rigidly defines the problem before anyone writes one line of code. In the real world things are fuzzier, and in many cases, nobody has a firm grasp on requirements.

Having worked for many years in commercial software development, I'm aware of problems encountered when using structured design tools. While I recognize the benefit of these tools, I am also aware that they often require I define the problem in more detail than I have.

Having had a long-time love affair with the Smalltalk language, I decided long ago to use it to prototype a user interface for a new contract. This contract had been very specific and it consisted of a piece of software with a user interface the client hated. Why did they hate it? Good question. What would they like in its place? Better question.

Given this vague definition, I decided that if I were to succeed, I would have to develop a series of alternatives. If I didn't, I'd be in the same position as the original interface designer and a new contractor would be seeing two interfaces the client hated. Realizing that my client couldn't afford to define their desirable interface by the process of elimination, I had to be able to work with them to determine why they didn't like the existing interface and to design one they would like.

Ah-ha. What a wonderful opportunity to use Smalltalk. If I was going to spend time developing many different interfaces, or endlessly fiddling with one, the last thing I needed to do was teach the machine basic algorithms over and over again.

This was my first successful rapid prototyping experience and it resulted in happy clients and happy developers. This book is not an academic exercise; it is describing a process I learned and have refined over several years. It works well because it was developed in response to the realities of real-world design.

Help

In this book, I discuss the solution of specific problems in very general terms. In my previous book, I dealt with specific issues of object-oriented design, but once again, my focus was the metal "gestalt" necessary to develop good object-oriented software, rather than specific coding details. Even though my book was basically about C++ programming, I had feedback from several programmers in languages such as Smalltalk and CLOS saying they felt the book was of value to them in learning the OOP paradigm.

On the other hand, there was a vocal minority that accused me of writing a thought experiment. I was somewhat offended by this, feeling that the book was more than a theoretical exercise. Over time I have become quite grateful that I did not publicly address these people because it turns out they were correct. The first book was unquestionably a thought experiment, and so is this one.

This book is a jumping-off point; therefore, I will try to make myself available to those of you who end up with new questions. I can be contacted at several electronic addresses. For those of you who own computers, but do not have access to a modem or a datanet, contact me through my publisher.

The easiest way to contact me is through America On-Line. The syops on this network have said that if there is enough interest they would be willing to spawn off a new area to support these discussions, allowing everybody to have a common area to communicate in.

Mark Mullin

America On-Line:	MarkMullin
Compuserve:	71410,1634
Applelink:	D4755 (attn: Mark Mullin)
Internet:	D4755@apple.com (attn: Mark Mullin)
U.S. Mail:	Mark Mullin
	c/o Addison-Wesley Publishing Co.
	5 Jacob Way
	Reading, MA 01867

CHAPTER 1

Software Development in a Computerized Society

In the fight between you and the world, back the world.

Today it is difficult to find anyone who would disagree with the statement that computers have radically changed our society. In the last 15 years they have permeated deep within the fabric of society, so that today we must interact with hundreds of them in our daily routines. From supermarket checkout systems and automatic teller machines to the endless store of facts that the government and credit agencies maintain on us, our lives are greatly affected by computers. From the lowly PC that runs the cash register at the corner store through the Crays that tell us tomorrow's weather, to the tens of thousands that allow us to reach across the miles and touch each other, computers have become the glue that holds our modern world together.

Traditional Design Methods Face Modern Needs

What we, as software developers, have apparently overlooked is that this has dramatically affected the way in which we do our jobs. Most of the "traditional" software design methods evolved in the 1960s and

1970s, and are primarily focused on the conversion of paper-based systems to electronic systems. In short, software design has been oriented more towards the replication of existing manual systems on computers than towards the complete redesign of those systems to account for what computers can really do. For example, many books on design use such things as inventory management, accounts payable, or similar tasks to show the design process. This means they also make the assumption that the software developer's task is to reduplicate an existing manual system, rather than create a new system from scratch (or to augment the behavior of an existing computer system).

Software developers are no longer confronting situations where they are reproducing manual systems. Now they are expected to replace a chunk of the client's middle management with an expert system, one that uses all of the system's existing data to decide such things as when to reorder, how much to reorder, what bills to pay, and what customers are good credit risks.

When we confront development requirements such as these, the clear problem definitions disappear. No longer can we look at a client's paper records and make electronic versions of them. We are no longer confronted with requests to take existing systems and computerize them; in fact, we are now making existing computerized systems "better-faster-smarter." To do this, we need to change some of our basic assumptions about how software is developed.

The first, and most critical, assumption we must change is that there is a clear definition of the problem. There isn't. When you are dealing with a client that wants to enhance their existing computer capabilities, you may be lucky enough to get a clear definition of the problem and be able to see an immediate solution. This is commonly called an *engineering change* and is simply an adaptation of the system to the client's particular way of doing things. If you expect to make your living by dealing only with problems such as these, don't expect to make a good living or even to be regularly employed. More often, a client will say something like, "Gee, this system has completely changed the way we do business. And now we have all of these great ideas about how we can get the system to do even more for us." Unfortunately, they can't give you a lot of detail about these new ideas. After all, that's why they hired you.

The use of computers has a strong effect on the organizations that use them, which is exactly how computers have managed to spread so far through society in such a short period of time. In the act of doing this, computers have altered the fundamental rules originally used to design software for them. Traditional design deals with moving existing tasks onto computers, it does not deal with the exponential growth in possibilities that comes after the moving has been accomplished. The new rules of design call for taking existing computerized systems and turning them from passive recorders of fact into active participants in the company.

As software developers we are therefore confronted by a problem. We have clients who are already computerized, who appreciate the added capabilities this computerization has given them, and who wish to extend this capability further. Unfortunately, they can't accurately describe all the aspects of the computerized system they are currently using, which makes it extremely difficult for them to specify their wishes. Describing the existing software is not enough, we must also define how the organization interacts with this software. When this synergistic combination is added to the design equation, we are faced with an explosion of information. We can't define the environment completely, therefore we can't define the project completely. We are forced to simply agree with the fact that it must do *more*, even though we can't fully define what *more* is.

So what can we count on? First, if the client feels that the software could do more to aid them, the fact that they can't define exactly what else it should do doesn't mean they are wrong. They interact with the system on a daily basis and are eminently qualified to make this statement. Second, while we can't assume the client can clearly define what it is they want, we can assume they can tell us what they don't want. Unfortunately, proof by negation doesn't work for design specifications. We can't create a design specification simply by getting the client to define everything they don't want; we would never be finished.

This means we must design knowing that the client cannot exactly describe their requirements, except in the most general terms.

A New Design Philosophy

As stated, we can trust our clients to realize when they need to expand the capabilities of their systems. We can also trust them to tell us when they don't like something about our new design, providing we present them with information about the design in terms they understand. Perhaps we can modify our design mechanisms themselves, so that we can successfully design new systems for our clients.

We all know, from painful past experiences, that clients don't understand traditional design walkthroughs. If they did, they wouldn't need us because they would be able to design and implement their own software. It isn't their job to be experts on design. If I had a nickel for every time a client has reacted violently to something I thought had been approved in a design walkthrough, I'd be living on a beach in Hawaii. However, this condition does indicate the path to success. When the client actually uses the software, they are always capable of forming a clear opinion about what they do and don't like. We should try to take advantage of this. If our clients can interact with the software while it is being designed and developed, we can catch problems quickly, before we have to throw a lot of expensive work out the window.

Design and Computer Aided Software Engineering

Much related work has already been done in this area, under the umbrella of Computer Aided Software Engineering (CASE). As software projects have become more complex, and correspondingly more expensive, a great deal of effort has been invested in formalizing the process of software development. This has lead to software development being treated as another concrete engineering discipline, although there are those who feel that this is a little premature, as well as a possible confusion of an art with a science.

In this effort to formalize software design, CASE tools have come to the forefront in the last few years. These tools are designed to work with the original software designers and systems analysts so that the final coding specification is both *correct* and *complete*. The hope is that when this point is reached, it is primarily a process of mechanical translation to move from the specification generated by the CASE tool to the final software product. Where a system design and its associated coding specifications used to be produced by some magical process known only to systems analysts, the systems analysts now feed all of their data about data structure, client requirements, and processing methods into the CASE tool, and the CASE tool magically comes up with the final specification.

There are three major problems with most existing CASE tools: they cost too much money, they still require a qualitative translation from the specification generated by the CASE tool to the final target system, and the tools are often extremely inflexible.

The first problem is easy to illustrate. The majority of CASE tools are designed to run on expensive workstations or minicomputers, and a hefty price tag is attached to the packages. Because of the formal engineering clothing they wear, they can also require expensive talent to operate them. Often, users must be conversant in the mathematics of programming, in such areas as pre and post conditions, invariants, and other formal program verification techniques. While these are invaluable utilities, they don't mesh well with the first phases of program design, when so much is already in flux. It's difficult to give a mathematically precise definition of a vague idea.

The second problem is slightly more difficult to illustrate, primarily because the problem is there in the first place. In simple terms, most CASE tools don't generate a specification in any kind of known programming language and because of this, they don't allow the end users to interact with the application program as it is being designed. What most CASE tools do is take in all of the formal parameters that govern a programs operation; for example, banking software should be aware of the difference between positive and negative account balances, verify that none of these conditions conflict with each other, and then produce a detailed specification that will be used by the programmers to implement the software. CASE tools generally guarantee that the final software will match the original design, but they don't spend too much time dealing with how that design is arrived at in the first place.

The third problem is best illustrated anecdotally. A year or so ago I was a contractor on a large software development project and watched as an analyst, after hearing from the clients that the data structures the analyst had defined were not what the clients actually used, recommended that the clients change their data structures. Obviously a laughable response, but one given with great deal of sincerity. From the analyst's point of view, it was probably easier to change the way the client did business than to argue with the CASE tool.

The basic problem here is that part of the CASE philosophy is very good and part of it is very bad. The good part is that we do need help from the computer during the design process and tools should be available to give us that help. The bad part is the assumption that the biggest problems with design arise because the process is not formal enough. This is a great academic reaction to the problem, but it doesn't work too well in the real world. In order to truly help modern software designers, the first things their tools must do is acknowledge that the initial design process is full of wrong starts and wild ideas. Flexibility is needed, not rigidity.

Design Languages

What is needed is a computer platform where programs can be created and modified interactively, a language which allows the program to be developed as it is designed. If we use a real programming language as the vehicle for expressing our design, we are guaranteed that the process of converting this program to the final environment is definitely one of translation—as we are only moving from one programming language to another. Likewise, we know we can solve our major problem of user interaction with the design, because if we use a programming language as the environment we design our software in, then we know the end users can "run" the design and can make valid judgements about its behavior.

This could be seen as a fairly radical proposal, insofar as commonly accepted software design principles state that one can only begin to implement a program in a computer language *after* it has been completely designed. In most languages this is quite true; to find flaws in the design during coding in a language such as Pascal or ADA, can result in expensive and time-consuming changes.

The reason we can't use an existing language such as Pascal to do the initial design is that we need far too much detailed information to simply sit down and start coding a program from notes on a napkin. The Pascal language is intended to implement programs efficiently, therefore it must stay fairly close to the architecture of the computer, in a general sense. A basic rule of thumb is that the higher the intellectual level of a language, the less efficient it is on the average computer. This really isn't surprising; LISP has never been recommended as a great real-time programming language.

The implications of this philosophy are where the real problems arise. If the intent of the language is to serve as an efficient vehicle for implementing algorithms on a computer, and it has stayed close to the machine to accomplish this, then we have made the designer responsible for moving the design a longer distance from the client's problem domain to the computer's problem domain. In short, the designer must do a great deal of translation, filling in all the little details necessary to go from the rather broad brush strokes of the client's problem description to the endless nitpicking required by the computer.

On the other hand, LISP is a high-level language that doesn't necessarily have this problem. We can construct and manipulate complex algorithms quickly in LISP, although we must admit that they are almost completely unreadable. But LISP still requires that we code all the elements of our design. We can't depend on LISP giving us any tools to allow us to quickly describe the common elements present in all programs. As a specific example, consider the fact that most common programs use standard data structures such as linked and keyed lists, sets of unique values, tables of information, and possibly a user interface based on windowing technologies. Every time we implement a program in LISP, we'll have to manually redefine all of this information, even though it deals with programming in general and not with the specific details of our design.

Given these observations, we can now define what we need in our new design tool. We want a high order language like LISP, where we trade the machine's efficiency for our own. Our programs will run more slowly, but we will write them much more quickly. We also want to be able to concentrate on the specifics of implementing our design so we want the computer to come pre-equipped with standard things that all programs do like manage blocks of data and user interfaces.

In the last five years, more attention has been paid to Object-Oriented Programming (OOP). OOP deals with the fact that programs are not developed in a vacuum, but rather, are built upon the shoulders of previous programs. An OOP environment traditionally provides a large library of classes, or basic program building blocks, which allows designers to concentrate on the application they are building, rather than the constant reimplementation of the traditional elements used in all programs.

What this means to the individual developer is quite straightforward. When you use an Object-Oriented Language (OOL), you expect it to already know about the basic organization of lists, arrays, and similar data structures. The system possesses templates by which to arrange these storage areas, and functions to perform standard operations on them. For example, many OOLs provide a Dictionary class, which allows the designer to associate an arbitrary piece of data with some key. There is no need for the designer to teach the system how to construct or manage a dictionary, it already knows how. If we needed to create a new dictionary object, and then place some data into it, we could simply state (in C++, an OOL related to C):

```
function(void* newKey,void* newData)
{
    // create a new dictionary object
    newDictionary = new Dictionary();
    //  add the new key/data pair
    newDictionary->addRecord(newKey,newData);
    // look up a key in the dictionary
    if(newData != newDictionary->lookup(newKey))
        print("Nahh. This can't happen!\n");
}
```

The main issue is that we could immediately decide we needed a dictionary to manage data retrieved by keywords, and then begin using it. We didn't have to spend time teaching the system how to manage a dictionary, it already knew how. The essentials of dictionary management don't change from application to application, so we can use this standard tool over and over again, in each program we develop. When we have a toolkit that includes hundreds of commonly used "smart" data structures, or *objects*, we are free to concentrate on the design of our application. Given the fact that this standard glue is usually much larger than the pure application logic, we can look forward to major decreases in development time. We can elect to teach the computer brain surgery by teaching it about the brain and what parts to cut, we don't have to start off teaching it basic motor skills.

Smalltalk

Given that we wish to use a high-level object-oriented language, the next issue is: which high-level object-oriented language?

Although I used LISP in the previous example and there is an excellent object-oriented extension for it (Common LISP Object System, otherwise known as CLOS), LISP is simply not the greatest language for design prototyping. Given that we know the prototype is to be written quickly and modified often, we don't need the extra problem of a language that can easily become unreadable. It isn't pure malice that makes some insist that the acronym LISP doesn't stand for LISt Processing, but for Lots of Irritating, Spurious Parentheses. Most importantly, LISP is a demanding system and is suitable only for large engineering workstations. It really isn't a good language for traditional PCs, as they just don't have the horsepower to run it.

We also can't use C++, as the standard implementation doesn't include a class library, meaning that although we have the capability to construct and reuse program building blocks such as dictionaries, we don't actually get them with the system. Additionally, C++ does make some efforts to be efficient in terms of execution speed and we've already discussed why this objective conflicts with the goals of rapid prototyping.

A language that does provide the high-level programming we need, possibly the largest library of predefined objects, and is available across a large range of PCs and mid-range machines is the Smalltalk language. Smalltalk is a very high-level object-oriented language developed by Adele Goldberg and her associates at the Xerox Palo Alto Research Center (PARC) during the 1970s and 1980s. Smalltalk is based on concepts originally developed in languages such as CLU and Simula, which are widely credited as the genesis points of the object-oriented programming paradigm. Smalltalk has become over time the archetypical OOL, and is the recognized basis of such systems as the Apple Macintosh computer and the Microsoft Windows programming environment.

Unlike its later relatives such as the Macintosh, Smalltalk was designed to allow for the rapid construction of complex programs, trading program efficiency for development time. The programmer is able to use a very high-level interpreted language, and it is the computer's responsibility to determine how to get from this high-level program to the bits and bytes the machine actually uses.

Smalltalk is available on a wide range of platforms, from the Digital Equipment VAX family and Sun Microsystem computers of every shape and size to the Apple Macintoshes and IBM-PCs under DOS and the Presentation Manager. There are two primary vendors for Smalltalk: ParcPlace Systems and Digitalk. A small Smalltalk package is also available as source code, in the semi-public domain (in the book *Little Smalltalk*, by Dr. Timothy Budd).

In *Rapid Prototyping for Object-Oriented Systems*, the specific version of Smalltalk used will be the Smalltalk/V Mac platform. The reason this platform has been selected is because it is relatively inexpensive, and the manual comes complete with an excellent tutorial. As the intent of this book is primarily to illustrate rapid prototyping, the tutorial will serve the readers well if any of the language details confuse them. Many of the basic concepts will work on either Digitalk or ParcPlace platforms, but if you are using ParcPlace, please be sensitive to some class differences between these systems.

The Client

The Schroeder trucking company has been computerized for many years, using standard packages and some custom work for billing their customers, generating truck logs and freight manifests, and other such information. As time has passed, Mr. Schroeder, the president of the firm, has noticed that with all the information they track about customers, trucks, and freight, they aren't really much more efficient than the competition when it comes to moving freight. Instead, their major advantage is just that they bill their customers faster, and they have a great after-the-fact database describing the freight they have shipped. What they would like to do is actively employ this mass of data at their disposal to make their actual freight handling more efficient.

Like many great ideas, this came to Mr. Schroeder in a flash as he heard an advertisement for an air express company, bragging about how their computer system could tell you exactly where your shipment was at any point between its origin and destination. Mr. Schroeder wondered, "if they can do that, why can't we make our computers figure out how to route our freight and load and unload our trucks more efficiently?"

Unfortunately, this exhausts the information Mr. Schroeder can directly provide you. Although he may very well be right, this is primarily a hunch for him, you are going to have to obtain the more detailed facts on your own.

Summary

This book discusses real design, with all its warts. To successfully design a system for your clients, you must first realize that they are clients, even if they think you're just another employee. Your job is to help them find out what it is they need *before* you begin to implement software. To accomplish this, you need to use tools which recognize that this process will be filled with fits and starts, so you aren't forced to commit to a particular plan too early in the development cycle.

In doing real design for real clients, academic abstractions such as structured analysis can often be more trouble than they are worth, at least until you have a clear idea of what the client wants. What you need to do is show the client a mockup of the system, rather than give them 50 pages of analysis they don't understand. If you use a language such as Smalltalk for prototyping, you know that whatever you do, it is both logical and computable, for the simple reason that you are doing it in a computer language. Paper products such as dataflow diagrams give no such guarantee because they are never subjected to the scrutiny of the computer.

Creating software is both an art and a science because it requires that you create something new from vague roots, and that whatever you create be logically complete. CASE tools can't really help you with the act of creation, as they simply automate the science of software production. The entire foundation of modern CASE tools assumes that you already have a clear idea of exactly what kind of system you will be implementing—this simply isn't the case in many modern software design tasks.

In short, successful design requires a good imagination, for you must be able to see the solution to the client's problem in your mind's eye before you can begin implementing this solution. Coupling this with a language that allows for extremely rapid software development means your imagination will always be controlled by the computer's capabilities, as you will have to translate your imaginings into Smalltalk code. When this is done, you have a concrete entity that both you and the client can work, and everybody is happy.

- Modern software systems are not analogs of previous manual systems, they are extensions of existing systems, and their foundation lies on the capabilities of computers, not on the capabilities of pieces of paper.
- Clients often have a vague grasp of their exact needs, therefore they cannot provide us with enough information to satisfy the requirements of traditional analysis methods. Clients do not do functional requirements!
- The best way to determine if a client likes a piece of software is to let them interact with it, and the worst way is to give them an analysis document.
- By prototyping a system and working with the clients through this process, the previous problems can be nullified.
- Smalltalk is a language where the development cycle is short enough that it can be used as a prototyping system.

CHAPTER 2

Designing Object-Oriented Programs

When you are sure you're right, you have a moral duty to impose your will upon anyone who disagrees with you.

This book assumes that you have a familiarity with the basics of object-oriented systems and understand components such as objects, classes, and instances. As we begin to analyze the problem and design our solution for it, we are identifying objects that already exist in the real world. This is one of the main strengths of Object-Oriented Design (OOD), the fact that components of a program are in many cases electronic realizations of entities that exist in the real world. For this reason, OOD can be seen as more of an expository process than traditional design methods, which are usually more synthetic. In short, it's usually easier to define something that already exists than to create something new from scratch.

When an entity that will be represented as a class in our prototype is mentioned, it will be shown with the first letter capitalized. You will notice that most of these classes are not initially enumerated for you in a table; instead, they are presented at the point of discovery, during the discussion of some aspect of the system. It it important you understand this process, for this is how you will find the majority of the application classes you will ever implement.

Preliminary Analysis

In beginning the analysis we must clearly state our objective. Whether we are extending the capabilities of an existing system, or creating a brand new system, we must understand what we wish to accomplish with our activities. Rapid prototyping allows for flexible development of software, but it depends on our having a specific objective. We know that Schroeder Trucking's basic interest is in streamlining their freight shipping. Our first task is to define exactly what that means and how the present systems help or hinder this process.

Starting with the simplest definition of the problem, Schroeder trucking deals with Customers who wish to move Freight from an Origin to a Destination. As I said, in Object-Oriented Program Design (OOPD), object-oriented systems are an electronic reflection of something that exists in the real world, either as a *concrete entity*, or a widely recognized *abstraction*. It would be peculiar if we were to implement some freight management software that did not include some type of Freight object.

In examining the software the company currently uses, we find it solidly traditional. Many of the concepts embodied in the software are drawn directly from the 1970s, with packages to do accounts payable, accounts receivable, and freight manifests. The current software's total contribution towards freight management is that if someone tells it all of the freight that is put on a truck traveling from point A to point B, the system will produce a manifest for the driver indicating this fact. The system is a passive recorder of facts and not an active participant in the job.

Surprisingly, this is a standard condition in many industries where they use computers to track what they are doing, but not to assume any active role in controlling what they are doing. Schroeder Trucking's current reaction is equally as common, as they realize that their computers know more about everything that's going on than do any of their employees, yet they do nothing to take an active role in this process. As far as the information they have at their disposal, the computer systems are the most qualified to make a lot of basic decisions about what should be done next. Yet they lack the capability to do this.

Before commencing our detailed research and design, we discuss this issue with Mr. Schroeder. Using extremely broad strokes of our design brush, we describe a new computer application that monitors all freight as it moves through the company's freight network. The system provides easy-to-use graphical interfaces for the foremen at the individual freight offices and works with them to help ensure all trucks are loaded as efficiently as possible. Using anecdotal descriptions, we detail how such a system could take into account the priority of various pieces of freight, the time they have spent in transit thus far, and how it could work with the foremen to make a decision to delay a particular truck for a day so that some inbound freight could be placed on the truck. By contrasting this with the way things now happen with two trucks being sent out half filled with low-priority freight, we can illustrate how such a system can achieve Mr. Schroeder's objective of using the available information to make the company more efficient.

With Mr. Schroeder's agreement, we now have managed to make our design goal a little clearer. Instead of simply agreeing that more could be done, we now have an agreement on *what more* can be done. We are going to implement a system that tracks all freight as it moves through the network and works with Schroeder Trucking employees to make the network function in as efficient a fashion as possible.

Returning to the world of software design in general, this kind of *target recognition* is the first step that needs to be taken. The client will recognize they have a problem, or that things could be better. From this, your first goal is to look at exactly what they are doing now and determine what the largest problem or shortcoming in their approach is. Once you have done this, use this information to immediately set a more detailed objective for what will be done. This doesn't mean you need to produce a formal proposal, simply that you must ensure that the following two critical facts are true:

- That you have correctly perceived a problem or weakness in the existing system.
- That you have correctly identified a workable solution to this problem.

Until you can establish both of these facts, there is little point in continuing. If you are the world's fastest rapid prototyper, without these facts established, you will simply produce the wrong prototype faster. Rapid prototyping offers great opportunity to decrease development time, but these time savings are based on the fact that you are developing the right system in the first place.

In working with clients, especially when the objectives are being discovered by mutual agreement, forget formal analyses. Nobody has time for them. It's not that they are unnecessary, but you are kidding yourself if you think there is enough concrete data for formal analysis. You should use anecdotal descriptions at this time. If you can paint a believable picture, as we did when we described the two half-empty trucks being replaced by one full truck, you can get a fast and accurate reading from the client on whether you understand the problem, and whether you have a solution for it.

Basic Objectives

Before we can begin to construct our prototype, we must determine exactly what information is available to us and what we can do with this information. Since our objective is to enhance the company's ability to efficiently move freight from origin to destination, we will examine the aspects of the current system that are related to this process.

We know that the system currently produces manifests for the truck drivers, indicating what freight is on their truck. Every piece of freight falls into one of three categories from the driver's point of view: those that they are actually delivering to a final destination, those that are being initially collected from a customer site, and those that are being delivered to the next freight handling facility to be moved to another truck.

Previously, we declared that Freight was moved from an Origin to a Destination. In examining exactly how this happens, we can describe other entities that are involved in this process. First, there are the various freight warehouses (Warehouse) that Schroeder Trucking operates around the country. Second, there are the trucks (Truck) that it uses to move this freight around. If we examine these entities, we can make several statements about how this system operates:

- Freight is either on a truck, in a warehouse, or waiting at a customer site.
- Freight moves from a customer site to a warehouse via a truck.
- Freight moves from a warehouse to a warehouse via a truck.
- Freight moves from a warehouse to a customer site via a truck.

The User Interface

The easiest way to define the overall characteristics of a program is to define the user interface for the program. All user interfaces have some type of operational focus which defines what the user interface, and therefore the program it is an interface for, is designed to accomplish. It isn't hard, for example, to recognize the user interfaces to such programs as text editors and spreadsheet managers.

In defining what kinds of information are presented and managed by the user interface, you define what the capabilities of the underlying program must be. While most traditional design is geared towards the development of the program first and the user interface second, this process is reversed in the rapid prototyping environment. The reason for this is simple. Your clients can interact with the user interface, even if it doesn't actually do anything. Core processing algorithms, on the other hand, are meaningless to them, regardless of the algorithms level of functionality.

The idea is that we construct the user interface, moving first from static displays of each of the main screens we expect to provide, through a *navigation* model, where a user can move from screen to screen, and finally to a detailed navigation model, where the interface is filled with as much detail as possible, allowing for the fact that there aren't really any routines supporting it.

By doing this we can work closely with a client during the process of designing the software, using the interface itself to help ensure that the final program is likely to satisfy the clients wishes. This is actually a traditional, top-down design approach; we have just placed the user interface higher in the hierarchy than the actual operations that the interface will carry out. The basic issue here is the definition of a user interface. A user interface, contrary to some popular thought, is not a set of code bolted onto the side of the application allowing the user to manipulate the application. Instead, a user interface is a window onto the application, where the user can look at the application as it runs and make changes to it.

There are two reasons that the Smalltalk language is good at rapid prototyping. The first involves the basic concepts about applications and interfaces embedded in the Smalltalk class hierarchy and the second, believe it or not, is because Smalltalk is such a good platform for top-down design.

Toy Interfaces

The Smalltalk applications model deals with views and models. A *view* is a component of a user interface, where the entire interface can be seen as a series of interlocked views presented on the screen. A view is divided into one or more *panes*, which are rectangular areas within each view used to display certain specific elements of data. A *model* is what a pane is looking at and is the real application if you will. For example, if we were to implement a simple interface that listed the freight items on a truck, then we would use a a view containing a single ListPane, and use a Truck as the model for this pane.

As you can see from Figure 2-1, this is quite a primitive interface, simply listing all the elements of freight in a truck. It doesn't even bother to tell us which truck it is displaying the manifest for. However, the implementation of this as a prototype is as simpleminded as the display we get.

Figure 2-1: A simple interface using freight items.

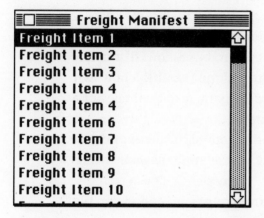

Examining a fragment of Smalltalk/V code for a moment, we would have actually constructed this pane via the following statement:

```
Truck::showFreight
    ListPane new
        model: self;
        name: #freightManifest;
        framingRatio: 0 @ 0 extent: 1 @ 1.
```

A ListPane is a class that comes with the standard Smalltalk/V system and is used to display and manage interactions with lists of information. It is a generic class that must be connected to the specific class it is managing data for via the model statement. As this ListPane is responsible for managing data for Truck objects, the code shown would be found in one of the instance methods in the Truck class. This means that the self parameter of the model statement is referring to the specific instance of Truck that invoked the method containing this code fragment. The name message is used to tell the ListPane how to get the data it will display. When the ListPane initializes itself, it will send the parameter given in the name message to the parameter given in the model message and use the Collection returned by this operation as the display data. In this example, when the ListPane starts, it will send the message freightManifest to the instance of Truck that is its model, and will display the data returned by this message.

This is an extremely flexible arrangement. We can define the behavior of the ListPane for all trucks that use it, but each ListPane can be connected to a different truck. In short, a simple mechanism which addresses the twin facts that all trucks display their data in the same way and that all trucks have different data.

We aren't ready to start defining our system to this level of detail yet, but it is important that you see how we separate the elements of the user interface from the application, or model. It doesn't matter whether we are listing items in inventory or freight on a truck. We manage the screen display the same way. The only difference is that we are looking at two different items, a Warehouse or a Truck. By plugging our model into these standard display management classes, by telling them who will give them the data to display and how to get them to provide this data, we can reuse these standard display classes in all of our projects.

Real Interfaces

We are ready to begin defining what our interface will look like, what objects will serve as models for it, and what messages these objects will respond to that will provide the data to be displayed in the interface.

Taking one of the simpler cases first, we know that there will be a requirement to inspect an individual piece of freight. In examining a piece of freight, we will want to know the following:

- the Schroeder code number assigned to this freight item (waybill number)
- the address the freight came from
- the address the freight is going to
- the freight's current location
- the next intermediate destinations of the freight
- the previous intermediate destinations of the freight
- the customer that shipped the freight
- the priority of the freight
- the day the freight was received
- today's date
- projected delivery date
- projected delivery time

Determining what parts of an object will actually be presented in a view is something of an art form, especially with more complex objects or views that simultaneously display more than one object. The best rule of thumb is to make the view display everything about the object that would be necessary to describe it on paper. For simple objects, such as this freight item, this can often mean displaying every piece of data carried within the object.

The next step is to decide how each of the items is to be displayed. To do this, we must examine each of the items in turn, and determine exactly what kind of data we will be displaying. The easiest way to do this, and provide ourselves with valuable future information, is to construct a table that lists each element along with the kind of data it contains and a brief note about the user's ability to change it. Table 2-1 shows what such a table for a Freight view would be.

Table 2-1: Example of a Freight view table.

Name	Data Type	Notes
Waybill#	String	Can't change
Origin	4 lines of text	Can't change
Destination	4 lines of text	Change, must keep original
Location	Truck or Warehouse	Can't change, but can switch to view of this item
Next Intermediate Destinations	Trucks or Warehouses	Can't change, but can switch to view of this item
Prev Intermediate Destinations	Trucks or Warehouses	Can't change, but can switch to view of this item
Customer ID	Customer	Can't change, but can switch to customer view
Priority	1 line text	Changeable
Date Received	1 line text	Unchangeable
Date Due	1 line text	Calculated
Time Due	1 line text	Calculated

As you can see, Table 2-1 roughs out the kind of data displayed for each element of the object and special comments about the user's interactions with the object. As stated, development of prototype software can often call for the interface to be developed before the true application objects. As you can see from this table, this isn't too bad as the interface tends to lead us by the nose to the application objects. If we are observant, the act of designing the interface will tell us a great deal about the application itself. After all, the interface and the application are closely related.

In the list of data types we have a series of entries, some of which have objects as data types. In building the interface, this has two important implications. First, we are going to have to pay special attention to the display of these elements, as there really isn't any one piece of data we can display. If we were displaying a string, that wouldn't be too hard. The only issues are: where's the string and where do we put it in the view? In displaying an object, things can get more complicated. Remember there are usually many ways to view the same object in one program, depending on the context in which the object is being displayed. There is no need to display a passing reference to an object in as much detail as that object's own view would do.

Second, in the case of the location, we know that freight can only be in one place at any time. This means that we will be displaying a string for this information, either the identification of the truck or the location of the warehouse. For the intermediate destinations, we will be displaying the same kind of data, as each of the elements on these lists has passed or will pass through the location field. When the Freight is initially accepted, we might generate the entire routing list for it. These destinations would all then end up in the *Next Intermediate Destinations* list. As the freight is transported towards its destination, the data would move from this list to the Location element and then, as the next destination was reached, the data would move to the *Prev Intermediate Destinations* list. From this we can deduce that while the location is a single line of text, the intermediate destinations will both be lists.

As for the Customer, we know that Schroeder Trucking, like all good companies, assigns each customer an utterly meaningless unique identifier that we will display in order to show which customer sent this freight. Who says everything can't be reduced to a number, or at least an alphanumeric!

As you can now see, even the simplest views can map over multiple objects. One would think that the information on a piece of freight would be straightforward and, as we can see, it is. But, an item of freight does not exist in a vacuum. Most application objects that you encounter will have links between themselves and other objects. Remember that the entire rationale of OOD is to distribute control throughout the system, breaking the system up into a collection of small interlocked objects. It is therefore reasonable to expect that many objects are going to contain references to other objects and because of this, the views of these objects are going to have to deal with those references.

We decided to adopt a very traditional approach and name the mapped objects in the Freight view. Instead of presenting information about the Warehouse or Truck that contains the freight, we simply show the name of this warehouse in our display. But what do we do if the user wishes more information? Let's say someone just realized that this piece of freight is a barrel of vinegar. They may wish to check the truck it is on to make sure there isn't a box of baking soda anywhere nearby.

The concept of *double clicking* (pointing the mouse at something and clicking a button twice in rapid succession) arose to deal with issues such as this. The concept doesn't really have to be tied to a mouse, you simply need a mechanism for saying "more information please" to the computer. In a mouseless PC environment, you could simply assign one of the function keys to this task.

When you have an area that is presenting information about an object referenced by the object being viewed, as with the Freight object referencing trucks and warehouses, it is considered to be a sign of good breeding to provide the user with a mechanism to switch to a view of the referenced object. The ability to switch from view to view by selecting components is called *navigation* and is critically important in a user interface. Too many windowing systems are built as pure trees, requiring the user to move back up the tree and down to another view to see information related to the first view. We aren't going to score any points doing that here because nobody wants to write down the truck number, go back to the main menu, select a truck view, and then type in the truck number they just transcribed off the screen.

In defining the Freight object view, we have identified the major data elements contained within each Freight object, and we have identified several other object views that will be linked to the freight view. Having done this, we can reproduce our table in more detail—see Table 2-2.

Table 2-2: Freight view table in more detail.

Field	Object	Edit	Nav	Note
WayBill#	String	O	O	Serves as Freight object ID
Origin	String	O	O	From Customer
Destination	String	O	O	From Customer
Location	Truck | Warehouse	O	X	From Route List
Next Int Dest	Trucks & Warehouses	O	X	From Route List
Prev Int Dest	Trucks & Warehouses	O	X	From Route List
Customer ID	Customer	O	X	From Customer
Priority	String	X	O	From a list
Date Recd	Date	O	O	From Customer
Date Due	Date	O	O	From Customer
Time Due	Time	O	O	From Customer

X = YES   O = NO

With this information, we can now decide exactly what the view will look like. The first thing that must be said is that the skills and techniques for designing a good user interface, vis-à-vis the arrangement of the data displayed within it, requires a set of skills that does not overlap the skills required to implement the interface. If you feel your artistic qualities are good, then forge on ahead whenever you are doing your own interfaces. If you feel they are questionable, then consult a friend or at least a good book on graphics design. As time passes and you prototype more and more interfaces, you will learn how to "read" your clients and prepare interfaces that they will like. In any case, be prepared to fiddle endlessly with the user interface. Once clients realize it can be changed around without much effort, change it they will. And more than once!

In any case, it's difficult to describe the exact rationale I use in laying out the views in the interface. There are some general rules I go by, as well as some methods I use to group the information in a view together. For now, I will lay out the Freight view, and then explain why I did things this way.

Since the Waybill# is the unique identifier for the freight item being viewed, we will dispose of it immediately by using it as the title

of the view. The origin and destination addresses, as well as the customer ID will be presented at the top of the view in the same form as
one might find them on a paper record such as an invoice. The priority and dates will be displayed under the address information. Then
we will display the current location in a larger type size under this,
and finally the previous and next destination lists. Given this, our display should roughly resemble Figure 2-2.

Before continuing, I should comment that in a few chapters, when
we actually implement this window, we are going to have to make
some changes based on what is easy to do in Smalltalk and what isn't.
This is not to say that the organization of the window will change,
simply a few cosmetic details. When you are initially designing a
view, don't worry too much about how you are going to implement it.
The initial design for a view should always assume the best of all possible worlds, where the language will do everything you want, within
reason. By this, I mean that you shouldn't worry about cosmetic details of the presentation, but on the other hand, you shouldn't assume
inordinately complex capabilities. The whole idea is that the design of
the view should be driven by the real requirements of the users of the
view, rather than the often capricious demands of the implementation
language.

The actual act of laying out the view provides you with another
set of information you will need in constructing the prototype. By deciding on the visual grouping of information in the view, you will also
be determining any data assembly, or aggregation, capabilities that
the view needs. If you look at where we have placed the priority and
date information, you will see that this information is logically
grouped together into a single area of the display. From the Freight
object's point of view, these items are all distinct and come from several different sources. From the view's point of view they are one unit.

Figure 2-2: The freight manifest.

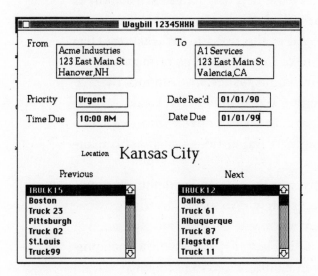

Not only does the view show you where you need to combine multiple data items together, it will also show you where you must decompose a single data item into several sections. We have been discussing the fact that we present three pieces of information about the location of the freight: specifically, its past and future destinations and its current location. Considering the underlying data for a moment, we can see that within the Freight object itself, this will most likely be implemented as a single ordered list of all destinations, with some reference to the freight's current position within that list. In the view, we have elected to split this list apart into three distinct units, to make the user interface more straightforward.

Summary

Even in the vague, unstructured environment of Rapid Prototyping, there are some rules to be followed, primarily concerning the *order* in which certain tasks should be performed. The first and most important step is that everybody agree on the driving *concept* behind the software. This concept doesn't have to be expressed in rigid terms, but neither should it be expressed in extremely vague terms. The idea is that the client and developers know *why* this software is being developed because they agree on *what* it is supposed to do when it is finished. In our case, we want to make our client's freight management more efficient by providing them with a system that can rapidly give them information about the freight they are moving. This allows us to focus our efforts in one specific area, as we can now assume we aren't responsible for understanding or upgrading things such as their invoicing system.

When this has been done, we can then begin to identify some of the primary elements within the system. When we determined that our objective was to implement a freight information system, we didn't have to make a giant intuitive leap to learn that the most important element within our system would be pieces of freight.

Once the overall objective of the system has been agreed on, and the central data element or elements identified, we can begin to pick apart the system in more detail. One assumption we can safely make is that all the important parts of the system will be connected in some way to this central data element. This isn't to say there won't be some parts hanging unconnected off the side, only that these unconnected parts aren't critical issues within the system. By beginning the process of identifying the connections between this central element and other elements within the system, we are beginning to flesh out the requirements of the system.

In conclusion, we must first reach consensus on what our overall objective is, and then we must identify the central elements that form this objective. We can then switch to a more expository mode, describing these elements in more detail, with each layer adding to our knowledge of the system's requirements.

- Before writing line one of code, developers and clients must agree on the *concept* of the new system. This doesn't require any kind of formal documentation, simply an agreement on what the system is supposed to do.

- Concepts are best described in anecdotal terms, as this ensures that everybody has the same mental model of the problem and the proposed solution to the problem.

- With the concept defined, one can then identify the central elements that form this concept. These elements correspond to the central *objects* in the prototype.

- By decomposing these central objects into their constituent parts, we can get a rough idea as to the overall complexity of the system because we can see the major interconnections between objects within the system.

- Scope out the user interface elements that will display the central objects. This isn't to say you will implement this interface right now, only that a picture is worth a thousand words.

- Describe the behavior of the central objects in the real world. The real-world behavior of the objects provides the model for implementing the software objects that mimic them. In short, freight objects within a computer operate under many of the same constraints as do freight items in the real world.

Exercises

In both of these exercises, the object is to describe what you expect the end system to be capable of, rather than designing its internal workings. In short, if we were living many centuries ago and attempting to invent a watch, we would be trying to describe what a watch will do for us, not the individual gears that it will use. We are interested in things like the face and the hands and how we will use it. We are not interested in the mainspring or the escapement.

1. Many software developers use one of the fancy time planners such as a Daytimer. If you are among this group, examine the different document forms that you use and determine your goals in creat-

ing a computerized version of this system. Then define the major elements of the system. You should find this to be a straight process of exposition, with individual classes describing the various types of pages in the planner, and another class serving as the notebook itself.

2. Examine your library of technical books and come up with the initial design of a system that would serve as a computerized reference to this library. Obviously, a Book is going to be the central object in the system.

CHAPTER 3

Some Reflections on Design

Merely because the group is in formation does not mean that the group is on the right course.

In the previous chapter we went through a rough process of analyzing the implementation of a window to display a freight manifest. While the exercise may have seemed premature, in the OOP design environment it is usually the fastest path to success.

Recall that I stressed the fact that you should view any OO program you write as a *system*. As in many systems, the average OO program contains a group of discrete objects that each perform a specific task and communicate with each other through some kind of network. Also, as in many systems, if you pop open one of the objects you will find the whole thing is repeated on a smaller scale, just like the nested dolls from Russia.

When you look at a program as a system you gain certain powerful advantages. Foremost, the overall reusability of your code becomes a joy to behold. By building a system from a collection of nested subsystems, the design will naturally divide between those classes that are application specific and those that are general purpose. You will find the construction of top-down structured programs not only easy, but natural in such an environment. You will also find that the overall structure of your system mimics that of the real-world system it is supporting or duplicating.

Dissecting the Design

Given this, the easiest way to implement any system is to cut through the system's skin, grab the first interesting part you see, and begin following the connections from that part to the other parts of the system. It is a process identical to the way we have learned about the human body. First, you have to cut into it. The skin is a barrier between the body's system and the external world. Any system has a skin because it is not healthy to allow the external world direct access to your inner workings, regardless of whether you are a body or an accounting program.

After you have made your incision, grab the first thing that looks interesting, learn what you can from it, but more importantly, find all the other widgets it's connected to. If we were dealing with the human body, we might find the stomach first. Not much help in understanding the brain you might say. Although you may guess that there must be a brain, you don't know if this is really the case. What you know is that most of the objects you will find in a system are there for a reason and are connected to other objects in the system. By starting off with a single object and following the connections through to other objects, you will end up with a very good map of how the system works. If you keep examining everything the stomach is connected to, you may arrive at the brain by following the path from the stomach to the lower intestine to the blood and then to the brain. That's only one of a great number of paths from the stomach to the brain, as any chronic dieter can assure you.

This process was reflected in the second chapter when we first identified the system's outward behavior, or skin. We decided to implement a freight management system. Then we selected one item we could quickly and accurately identify as a component of it and investigated how it worked; we used the freight manifest to do so.

While doing this, we are identifying other objects in the system like brains and warehouses, but we don't immediately define exactly how these objects act. In OOPD we aren't discarding the learning of the past which has served us well—specifically structured design as personified by people such as Edward Yourdon and Michael Jackson. If anyone tells you that structured design has nothing to do with OOP, avoid them like the plague. The real contribution made by all OOP languages is that the top-down structure of the design is concretely manifested in the final program, in terms of the objects implemented and their relations between each other. Structured design is much easier and more natural in an OOL than it is in a traditional language and, not surprisingly, it works better.

In defining objects, we take advantage of top-down structured design at every opportunity. If you had the Herculean task of writing a program to precisely duplicate all functions of the human body, you would start off with a Brain object. You would be well aware of the fact that there would most likely be tens of thousands of objects necessary to support that object, but you'd only worry about them when you'd defined all the large objects, like stomach, lungs, and a heart. From another view, imagine the construction of a house, where first they lay the foundation, put up the walls, the roof, and then they go to work on the inside of the house. There's little point to putting up the internal walls without the roof because they will just be ruined by rain. Putting up the internal walls before the foundation Is only possible when building poor software.

In any case, we dug into the requirements, found out our basic objective, and began to cut into the system to see how it worked. In doing this, we were constantly asking the question: *How does the existing system work?* This is a vital question in design, but one that some designers translate to another form, namely the statement, *This is how the system works*. In other words, instead of designing the system from an existing model, they design a new one from scratch. There are two major flaws with this approach. The first is that they aren't getting help from the existing real-world system in understanding how it works. The second is that when they are all done they will have to hammer the real world into a new form so that it can use their new system. The end result is that the people who arbitrarily announce how a new system will work cost themselves a great deal of extra work and antagonize their user community (assuming they succeed in the first place). Many zealots who make this proclamation seldom make it a second time.

The best way to do OO program design is to realize that you are dealing with systems and the best source of information is the system you are duplicating or enhancing. Your job is not to dictate how the system will work, but to understand how the system already works. As you do this, you are acquiring valuable information about the classes you will need to construct your system and how instances of these classes interact with each other at runtime. In more formal terms, most systems are defined in terms of structure and communication. Structure, to an OO programmer is the definition (variables and methods) of the classes that were used to construct the system. Communication is defined by the runtime messages and data packets that pass between objects in the system. When you have both elements defined, you have everything necessary to build your program.

Continuing the Design

From our work in the previous chapter, we identified three major classes that are connected to a freight manifest. The classes, Truck, Warehouse, and Customer, are all specialized classes that we identified in Chapter 2, but did not implement.

The decision on which class to implement next is a subtle but important detail in OOP design. There are many possible orders in which you can choose to implement your classes, but some orders are better than others. OOP is very different from traditional program-

ming in this, primarily because OO programs are top-down structured programs at their very core, whereas traditional languages only
pay lip service to the top-down design principles. In a traditional language it doesn't matter how you build a large application because
each module is effectively built in a vacuum and then they are meticu-
lously hand threaded with each other to build the final program. OO
programs, on the other hand, are built within an "environment" which
is primarily defined by the class hierarchy. Through this, all OOP
modules, or classes, are defined in terms of the OOP classes that existed before them. This is done by classes descending from an existing
class, inheriting some capabilities from their base classes, and by mu-
tating other capabilities so that they can now be defined in terms of
their differences.

This has certain immediate implications concerning the order in
which the elements of the design for an OO program should be defined. The most obvious is that you should not begin to implement a
subclass if you don't know what its base class is.

The more subtle, but valuable implication deals with the order in
which you should define your classes. By considering the classes you
have designed so far, you should always select new classes by finding
the next candidate that will help you define the largest number of
new requirements. For example, if we had decided that in addition to
the three classes previously mentioned, we also needed to implement
a String class, we aren't going to design the String class next because
its design will give us very little new information about the system in
general. Likewise with the Customer, as it's not really related to the
system's prime function of tracking freight. This leaves us with the
Truck and the Warehouse. In this case, Warehouse is the most likely
candidate because a Warehouse deals with many Trucks, but a Truck
deals with two Warehouses at most. When confronted by two or more
objects that could all be designed next, pick the one that refers to the
largest number of external objects. Statistically speaking, it's the one
that will probably give you the most new information.

Now that we have decided to design the Warehouse next, we must decide whether we will implement the class or the class's view next. This is almost always an easy decision. You usually implement the view first.

The reason for this is simple and rooted in human nature. When we seek to understand anything, we tend to draw a picture of it. When you try to define a class you are most likely going to first try to draw a picture of it. Well, if you need a view and the view is effectively a picture of the class, why not just design the view first? This shouldn't be a soul searching question, just one that asks if you might learn a little more about the object by figuring out how to display its contents first.

OOP design is like a game of strategy in that you attempt to maximize your opportunities at all times and you always look for the simplest thing that will pay off with the most benefits. You cut into the system you are examining and grab the first thing you see. By attempting to define the object that you are examining, you will inevitably define some of the objects connected to it. From there, you keep defining the object that will give you the most new facts about the system. When you have finally exhausted all of the objects you have recognized as components of the design, you have finished your decomposition of the problem.

The Runtime System

One problem I have found in OOP design is that there has been relatively little effort to define the taxonomy of runtime OOP systems, although great effort has been spent on the class hierarchy concept. However, there is wide agreement that class hierarchy cannot by itself be sufficient.

To see the problem clearly, consider the view we defined in Chapter 2 and how we said that the view of a Freight object used internal references to Truck and Warehouse objects. The existing structure within the OO development environment is the class hierarchy, which defines a static network of classes with all the connections based on the shared operational characteristics of each class. In short, the more closely classes resemble each other, the more closely together they are found in the class hierarchy. We have a rough idea of where these three classes sit in the hierarchy and they are only distantly related. It is while the system is running that their relationship becomes closer, but the running system is organized along a whole different set of principles. Instead of classes being grouped statically by their structural and functional relationships, classes or instances of these classes are related based on the tasks they are performing.

Technically, we are looking at the difference between inheritance and delegation. *Inheritance* is a static relationship whereby classes are hooked together in a hierarchy based on their overall similarity to each other. *Delegation*, on the other hand, is a dynamic relationship where a particular class will delegate one of its responsibilities to a more specialized class to which it holds a dynamic reference. One of the simplest examples of this is a class that needs to maintain a list of sorted values. There is no need to reimplement a sorting function to do this or even to make a special effort to call one. Instead, we would simply define the variable we wish to hold the value as a Sorted-Collection, which would automatically sort data placed into the list. Through this we have delegated the responsibility for sorting the list to a specialized object, to which we hold a dynamic reference.

In analyzing and defining the system you discover structural and dynamic information in parallel. You have seen how we define the static relations between classes by where we locate each new class in the hierarchy. You have also seen how we define the runtime system, primarily in terms of what specific objects are linked together in order to perform some task.

Defining the Warehouse View

Now that we have settled on designing the WarehouseView class next and have defined all of our reasons for doing so, we can get down to the actual design of the class itself. Once again, the first step is simply to think about a picture of a warehouse and how one would interact with the warehouse.

In doing this the first thing we can say is that a Warehouse contains two things of great interest. It contains a list of all the freight stored in that warehouse and a list of all the trucks in the warehouse, including those that have just left or are about to arrive. Additionally, we know from the Freight view that each warehouse has a name, which is the city the warehouse is located in.

We have now exhausted what our previous design work has already indicated about warehouses. The next step is to consider the warehouse at a deeper level so we can get information on things that are important to Warehouses, even if they aren't directly important to freight management systems.

A warehouse isn't built around a black hole, so it has some limited capacity in freight. Therefore, a warehouse will track two values: its total capacity in freight and the amount of that capacity which has already been used. Examining this, we realize that freight sizes will probably be expressed in cubic feet. That's no problem for the new Warehouse class, we just add two new variables with three element arrays that can hold the length, width, and height measurements. But what about the Freight class? This means we need to have the freight object carry its dimensions and we already designed it without dimensions!

This is a natural part of OO design, you will often find future work indicating that something you did previously isn't quite sufficient. It isn't a big deal, it happens all the time. You simply extend the previous design to encompass the new requirement. When we get deeper into the coding, you will see how a system such as Smalltalk can aid you in this, making the process ridiculously easy.

When this does occur; however, there is one quick check you should always make. If the change to an existing class design is augmenting it to make up for something it originally lacked, then go ahead and make the change. If, on the other hand, you are changing the way the class used to do something, stop and examine the situation closely. These actions would indicate that the previous design was not lacking some capability, rather it was doing something wrong. When this occurs, you will often find changes will have to be made all over the system, as it reflects a flaw in the existing design to this point. Try to avoid situations like these, they can ruin your day.

Returning to the Warehouse, we can see that we don't have to worry much about the changes to the Freight class and the corresponding view, as the addition of a freightSize variable is straightforward. Continuing with our examination, there doesn't appear to be anything else that is vitally important to defining a Warehouse. Admittedly, there are all sorts of nice things we could do, like transit and loading statistics, but we can focus on that later. When designing an OO system, you should always leave capabilities contained within a single object to the later stages of the design. In this case, we could implement nice statistical functions for a Warehouse, but that won't tell us too much about the rest of the system.

Reviewing the items we have identified, we end up with this list of elements we should display in the view. After analyzing the elements and determining their interactions, you should be able to construct an accurate display list for the Warehouse view. The list should look something like Table 3-1.

Table 3-1: The Warehouse view.

Field	Object	Edit	Nav	Note
freightStored	List/Freight	O	X	List of Freight contained in Warehouse. Double click takes you to the freight manifest view.
trucks	List/Truck	O	X	List of Trucks at the Warehouse. Double click to view truck.
inbound	List/Truck	O	X	List of Trucks coming to this Warehouse. Double click to view truck.

Field	Object	Edit	Nav	Note
outbound	List/Truck	O	X	List of Trucks that just left this Warehouse. Double click to view truck
capacity	3 Integers	O	O	Gross Capacity of this Warehouse, in cubic feet.
used capacity	3 Integers	O	O	Number cubic feet capacity used by freight currently in the Warehouse.
name	String	O	O	City in which this warehouse is located.

From this information, we can proceed to design the Warehouse view. We know from Table 3-1 that the view will display four lists of information on the warehouse contents, trucks in the warehouse, and the trucks that are due to arrive or have just left. Additionally, we'll need to display some header information about which warehouse this is and how much room it has left in it. Given all this, the display in Figure 3-1 should be adequate for these purposes.

As it turns out, the Warehouse view didn't show us the presence of any new classes. But we did learn some interesting things. We learned that there is a loop between the Freight object view we designed in the second chapter and the Warehouse view. In the Freight view a double click in the city field will bring up a Warehouse view and a subsequent click over the freight item in the Warehouses freightStored variable will return the original Freight view.

We are also starting to see enough of the system to recognize that the three most important elements within it are Trucks, Warehouses, and Freight. Everything else in the system exists purely for their convenience. This is an important event in the development lifecycle of an OOP system, because it marks the first time you see the application as a complete system. When you begin to describe a system as a series of essential interactions between major units within the system, that is a good sign that you have moved from simply seeing the system's external actions to understanding the system's internal operations.

Figure 3-1: The Warehouse view with header.

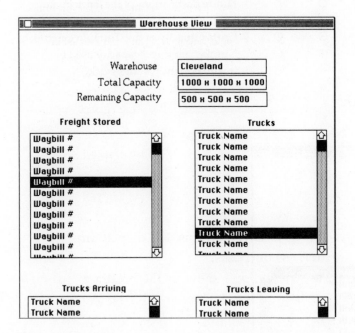

The Truck Class

We once again examine the characteristics of the object we are defining, a truck, and find that it contains four elements of interest. They are shown in Table 3-3.

The window isn't too hard, something like the one in Figure 3-2 should do nicely.

Table 3-2: A Truck's Characteristics.

Field	Object	Edit	Nav	Note
id	String	O	O	Unique identification of this truck.
onboardFreight	List/Freight	O	X	List of Freight contained in Truck. Double click takes you to the freight manifest view.

Field	Object	Edit	Nav	Note
route	List/Truck	O	X	Future destinations of the truck in order of arrival.
capacity	3 Integers	O	O	Gross Capacity of this Truck, in cubic feet.
usedCapacity	3 Integers	O	O	Number cubic feet capacity used by freight currently in the Truck.

Figure 3-2: Window for a Truck.

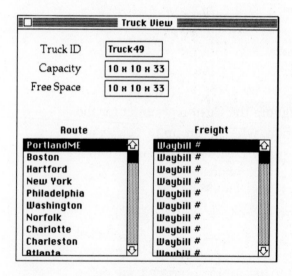

The Reference Network

The references we have established between the views gives us valuable information about the ways in which the Warehouses, Trucks, and Freight are related. By assembling a table of all the references between views we can construct a network that shows us how these elements are constructed. Table 3-3 lists the references.

Table 3-3: Relations between Warehouses, Trucks, and Freight.

View	Refers to View	Through
Freight	Truck	location, route
Freight	Warehouse	location, route

View	Refers to View	Through
Freight	Customer	customer
Warehouse	Freight	freightStored
Warehouse	Truck	trucks, inbound, outbound
Truck	Freight	onboardFreight
Truck	Warehouse	route

Figure 3-3 shows us many things about the internal behavior of the system we are building and will be invaluable in our next phase of design. Here, we shall simply examine the network to see what holes in our knowledge it fills in.

The first obvious conclusion is the Customer object is definitely going to be a dead end in the system, as it is only referenced by Freight objects. The next obvious conclusion is that this is a classic three-element star network, if we ignore the Customer object for the time being. This kind of configuration, where a group of objects are tightly interlocked in a network, usually indicates the existence of a meta-object, which is a pure dynamic object, one for which there is no static class definition. A meta-object is formed from multiple objects and implements an outside behavior for all other entities in the system to interact with. Using a biological example, the actual defined classes that compose the elements of the meta-object for the nucleus of a cell, the integration of which forms a meta-object that behaves like a complete cell.

It really isn't surprising that we found this particular meta-object, as it's the system itself. When we run an OO program, we are interacting with all the objects in the system. After all, that's what the system is there for. By definition, the cooperative operation of a group of objects forms a meta-object, which provides a transparent, higher level interface to the objects it maps to. Sounds suspiciously like the definition of an application program to me.

Figure 3-3: The internal behavior of a system.

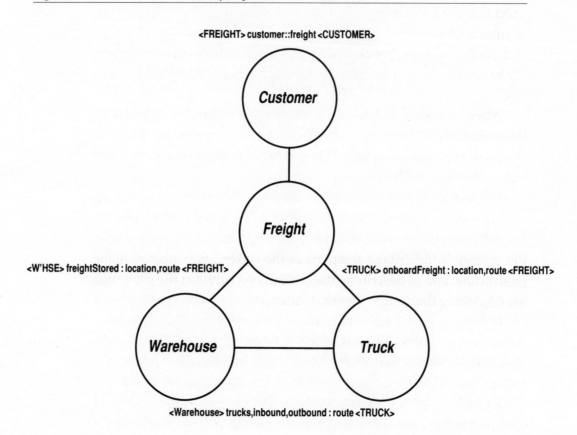

<FREIGHT> customer::freight <CUSTOMER>

Customer

Freight

<W'HSE> freightStored : location,route <FREIGHT>   <TRUCK> onboardFreight : location,route <FREIGHT>

Warehouse   **Truck**

<Warehouse> trucks,inbound,outbound : route <TRUCK>

Summary

Most systems you will encounter, both physical and abstract, have a *skin*, or *boundary*, which defines the boundaries of the system itself. In order to understand any system you must dissect it, which means that your very first task is to cut into the system and peel back the skin so you can see what is underneath. The boundary of any system also clearly defines the separation between the user's viewpoint of the system and the system implementor's viewpoint of the system. The user is on the outside and looks at the skin of the system as the whole system. The designer, on the other hand, is on the inside and looks at the parts that are contained within the system as the whole system. Returning to the watch example, to the user of a watch, the hands and face are the system. To the designer of a watch, the gears that drive the hands are the system, and the hands simply reflect the state of this system.

When you begin to dissect a system, you can assume that most of the parts of the system are connected to each other in some way. This means your analysis can be fairly flexible, you can assume that as you follow the relationships from one part to another, you will finally succeed in understanding what all the parts do. Therefore, as you dissect the system, you attempt to describe the largest parts you see, preferably those that have the largest number of connections to other parts of the system. In describing the parts of the system, you are describing its *structure*, and in describing the connections between the parts, you are describing the system's *communications*.

In designing an OO system, you need to be aware of the difference between runtime and compile time issues, issues which are most clearly described in the difference between *delegation* and *inheritance*. Delegation is a runtime issue, where an object uses another object to accomplish some specific task for it. It is not necessary that these objects be directly related to each other in functional terms, only that the delegating object has a requirement for a certain task to be performed. Inheritance, on the other hand, deals with *static* relationships between classes, allowing one class to inherit the capabilities of a class it is related to.

- Systems have a skin, which is roughly equivalent to a user interface.
- You define a user interface by describing the skin.
- You can't determine how a system works until you peel back the skin.

- Systems contain distinct parts, which give them structure. These parts communicate with each other to make the entire system work together as a single unit.
- Systems are recursive, so what appears to be a structure within a system can easily be a new system in its own right.
- Systems are defined in terms of their inheritance (or genetic relationships between structural building blocks), and in terms of their runtime cooperative activities, those tasks they delegate to specialized units.
- If you have the opportunity, implement a *viewer* for a specific object before you try to directly implement the object. Human nature being what it is, a picture is usually worth 10^3 words.
- Don't forget to keep track of the communications network that links the structural elements of the system together. Although in OO systems it isn't directly manifested in procedural logic, the communications between objects is as important as the definitions of the objects themselves.

Exercises

1. Design a simple checking account manager. Concentrate on the *views* of the various objects within it.
2. Define the *structure* and *communications* between the keyboard, monitor, disks, and CPU of the average personal computer. You don't have to simulate one, just define the parts and how they communicate with each other.

CHAPTER 4

Developing the Skeleton

Measure it with a micrometer, mark it with a grease pencil, and cut it to fit with an axe.

We have now defined enough of the major operational units in the system to construct our first operating prototype. By implementing our designs for the Freight, Warehouse, and Truck objects, we can construct an operational prototype—one that we can actually sit down and use, albeit to a limited extent. To accomplish this, I will be presenting some Smalltalk code without explaining all of its internal details. If you are new to Smalltalk, I recommend you keep a reference book handy.

Unlike traditional development, rapid prototyping is not based on a linear path from design to development. Instead, development is tightly intertwined with the design. The first objective in designing for the RP environment is to produce a stable core onto which the rest of the design can be hung. As soon as this core has been designed, as we have done with our central classes, it should then be implemented as a prototype. After this has been accomplished, as the design fills in the details, the prototype can be modified to account for the changes, *allowing the design and prototype to constantly reflect each other.* As the design changes, so does the prototype and as the prototype changes, so does the design.

The first step in implementing our prototype is to decide on what specific things we are going to implement. From our design we know we will need the basic classes Truck, Warehouse, and Freight. Additionally, we will need the corresponding TruckView, WarehouseView, and FreightView classes to support the views of each of these objects.

Core Classes

In designing these core classes, we want to remember that they form much of the skeleton on which we will be *hanging* the remainder of the system. Although we shouldn't be overly concerned with getting everything perfectly right the first time, it is important that we don't do something really strange at this point. If we were to do something bizarre, we would have to deal with the effects of it throughout the rest of the prototyping process. It is very important to ensure that core classes within your prototype are as natural as possible, for their organization will have great impact on the organization of the classes to be implemented in the future.

This is an example of another relation between classes, one which you should be aware of, one that is not reflected in the class hierarchy itself. The core classes affect the classes to be defined in the future because they are the foundation on which these classes operate, not because they form part of the physical definition of these future classes.

Freight Class

The freight class, as defined in Chapter 2, contained the following variables, as shown in Table 4-1.

Table 4-1: Freight class variables.

Waybill#	String
Origin	4 lines of text
Destination	4 lines of text

Waybill#	String
Location	Truck or Warehouse
Next Intermediate Destinations	Trucks or Warehouses
Prev Intermediate Destinations	Trucks or Warehouses
Customer	Customer
Priority	1 line text
Date Received	1 line text
Date Due	1 line text
Time Due	1 line text

We can see that the Freight class will be a direct descendant from the Object class because it isn't closely related to any of Smalltalk's standard classes. The first decision, after deciding which object is to be implemented, is to determine where it goes in the class hierarchy. This decision is critical—as a poor choice can cause you many problems; a good choice can save you a great deal of work. The principle is simple: always attempt to find the superclass that does most of the work for you. If you wanted to create a Stack class, you'd use an existing Collection class, as stacks are a kind of collection. Therefore, the existing collection classes are likely to have already implemented methods you are going to need. Deriving the Stack class directly from the Object class would mean that you would have to redevelop many features the collection classes already provide.

Given that we know what data is contained within a freight object and we know where the freight object goes, we can proceed with creating the class. Using the New Class menu command, create the Freight class with this definition:

```
Object subclass: #Freight
  instanceVariableNames:
   'waybill origin destination location
      nextIntermediateDestinations prevIntermediateDestinations
      customer priority dateReceived dateDue timeDue '
  classVariableNames: ''
  poolDictionaries: ''
```

To operate the freight object, we must first implement methods for certain functions that we expect all classes to be able to perform. The first group involves the *construction* and *destruction* of objects, the second involves *access* to data within objects, and the third consists of those functions which are truly *specific* to a particular class. Whenever you begin to implement new class, you can always divide the functions it will need into these three categories: control that initializes, destroys, and otherwise plays with objects; access that provides methods for outsiders to access and possibly change values within the object; and functions that provide all the methods the class was originally designed to implement in the first place, before all these petty bookkeeping details were introduced.

In construction and destruction functions we must provide a new class method to ensure that the initialize instance method is invoked for any new instance. This guarantees that all new instances of the class are properly initialized. This is more of an issue in Smalltalk than in C++, as C++ provides for the existence of initialization methods that are automatically called when a new instance of a class is created. Smalltalk, on the other hand, does not automatically call an initialization function, so you must override the new method to do so.

To accomplish this, we add the class method new to the Freight class, making it trigger the execution of the instance method initialized for every newly created class. Between these two functions, the new Freight class has now been integrated into the system's initialization sequencing. This technique applies to every class you implement that requires any kind of custom implementation.

```
new
    ^super new initialize

initialize
    nextIntermediateDestinations := OrderedCollection new.
    prevIntermediateDestinations := OrderedCollection new.
    ^self
```

After satisfying the system's environmental demands, it is now important to deal with the interface between the object being designed and the other objects that will be using it. This interface is primarily implemented by the access functions, which are used to move values between the Freight object and external objects.

From the code for the initialize method, we can see that the system's version of an initialization statement is not really an initialization statement from our application's point of view. Our application isn't even aware of what the initialize function does, as it only sees the results. Our application, however, has very specific ideas about what constitutes a legally initialized Freight object, and the methods that do this are the next to be implemented. The first access functions we will implement will set and return the basic data required for each freight item.

In the following function, which initializes a new Freight object with required data, two new class variables are introduced. The WayBillCounter is provided to allow the system to automatically fill in the waybill field of each new Freight object with sequentially ascending numbers. The MasterManifestLog is a dictionary where all newly created Freight records are stored, using their waybill number as retrieval keys. One thing that this method does show us is the minimum amount of data we must have from an external source to create a new freight object. At the very least we must know who is sending the freight, where they are sending it to, and precisely when they expect it to arrive.

```
origin: aString destination: aString customer: aCustomer dateDue:
aDate timeDue: aTime
    origin := aString.
    destination := aString.
    customer:= aCustomer.
    dateDue := aDate.
    timeDue := aTime.
    waybill := WaybillCounter.
    WaybillCounter := WaybillCounter + 1.
    MasterManifestLog at: waybill put: self.
    ^self
```

That's the initialization the application needs to have done for each freight object, and that has shown us which parts are system generated, which are optional, and which must be defined. The parts that are optional or will be computed later, such as the priority and the intermediate destinations, can be ignored until later. The parts we had to initialize, such as the customer, have been initialized and are have therefore become boring and dull. On the other hand, the system-generated waybill, as well as the sudden addition of manifest tracking activity, might be interesting.

When constructing initial prototypes you will often find that you discover the requirements for global variables in the process of implementing member functions for a class. Don't fret, this doesn't mean you are a sloppy analyst. If I were to analyze a problem down to the level at which I had established relationships between the numbering of the paper manifests and a global variable for numbering the electronic manifests, I could only observe that I had generated far too much paper for far too little a program. I wish I could live long enough for an analysis that detailed to be completed. Expect to encounter requirements for new global variables throughout the prototyping process.

In this case, the class definition was changed to add the new global variables and a new class method, resetSystem, was added. The resetSystem method is intended to be used whenever the entire system is to be reset, in effect purging the system and starting it anew. Great care should be exercised with such functions. While they are absolutely necessary for bootstrapping your design, if they sneak into the final systems you will be handing your user a loaded gun where a single command can destroy all of their data.

Clearly you are building a prototype of your application. But not even this prototype can start from a complete void, so you are also implementing very destructive functions such as resetSystem which have the ability to directly alter the core environment. Functions like resetSystem are not truly part of the prototype but they are necessary during the design process to help establish the environment in which the application will operate. After the application is operating to your satisfaction, you must remove all of these support functions. If you leave them around, you will regret it one day.

Let's return to the immediate case of the dangerous environment function we created for the freight object. The code for this function, as well as the modified class definition, appears below:

```
Object subclass: #Freight
 instanceVariableNames:
  'waybill origin destination location
     nextIntermediateDestinations prevIntermediateDestinations
     customer priority dateReceived dateDue timeDue '
 classVariableNames:
  'MasterManifestLog WaybillCounter '
 poolDictionaries: ''

resetSystem
  WaybillCounter := 1.
  MasterManifestLog := Dictionary new.
```

Our next task is to implement all of the methods that will allow external objects to access the instance values of the Freight object. We will elect to implement access methods for every variable *except* the two intermediate destination lists. The rationale for this decision is that all of the other objects are usable by themselves, whereas these two lists are built for and maintained by the Freight class. It seems reasonable to assume we will implement higher order functions to return information from these lists. In one fell swoop, we implement the following member functions:

```
waybill
  ^waybill

origin
  ^origin

destination
  ^destination

location
  ^location

customer
```

```
^customer

priority
   ^priority

dateReceived
   ^dateReceived

dateDue
   ^dateDue

timeDue
   ^timeDue
```

As you see, these functions are extremely straightforward and a little drab. In systems developed after Smalltalk, many programmers had elected to allow anyone to directly reference elements within an object on a read-only basis. This means that every class inherently provides a means to access the values of each of its instance variables. There are those who argue that this is dangerous, since access to an object's instance variables, even read-only access, should only be granted by the specific direction of the programmer. Speaking as a hassled programmer, I'll take my chances. Saving an hour on a regular basis not working on the read access methods for a class for the problems involved in reading the wrong value once in a while sounds like a deal to me.

After implementing the read access functions, we can begin to consider the write functions or what potentially dangerous things we are going to allow outside objects to do. Considering it, we decide that since we are just starting and don't know very much, and the fact that we can always add stuff later, we aren't going to allow very much now! This is usually the safe decision, as it's always easy to add a missing method later, whereas it's very hard to undo the effects of trashing an integral object within the system, except by writing more dangerous methods to undo the effects of the first dangerous method. We decide (as it's really a function of the difference between today and the date a piece of freight is to be delivered and since neither of those two values can be modified) that we will graciously allow outside objects to directly modify the priority value. Therefore, we need to add the following instance method to the Freight class definition:

```
priority: aPriority
  priority := aPriority.
    ^self
```

Balancing Class Development

We have now taken care of the glue which is necessary in an object-oriented program running on a computer, but not necessary in the pure world of freight, trucks, and warehouses. We must implement at least a minimum amount of this glue code first whenever we create a new class because we need to connect the class to the objects around it. It can't function until we do because it doesn't have any way to get input or deliver output.

I stated previously that it is usually easier to design an object's view first in order to understand the object better, with the justification that a picture is worth a thousand words. Now, when we actually get to writing code, you see that I have implemented the actual object code before I have implemented its view code. The reason behind this has to do with the way object-oriented systems are constructed, especially prototype systems.

In building an OO system, you want to develop the classes in parallel so they possess the same relative degree of sophistication. This isn't to say that all classes should end up at the same level of complexity, rather, it means you shouldn't add to the capabilities of one class when another class that uses it is greatly inferior. If you were a genetic engineer and you wanted to build a team from one modern man and one Neanderthal you would probably make changes to the Neanderthal before changing the modern man. You want to make them more equal and it seems stupid to make the modern man more like the Neanderthal so you make the Neanderthal more like the modern man.

Returning to computer-oriented cases, the classes already present in Smalltalk, which support views, know a great deal more about life than does our new Freight class. The view classes can already fetch, process, and display data, whereas our Freight class just learned that it actually had data. At this point, having created the glue routines that allow an external object like a view to look at the variables in a freight object, we could implement a simple view. Before the glue, any work we did on the view would be untestable until we had created the glue. Therefore, when building any OO system, pay attention to the relative sophistication of the various classes involved. The first task in implementing any object is to add enough glue so that the rest of the classes in the system can use it.

The View

Having implemented the glue methods, we can now implement a view of the Freight object. This view will be very simple at first, just showing the contents of each of the variables in a Freight object (see Figure 4-1).

Reviewing the window design presented in Chapter 2, we find that in order to implement this window we will need two ListPanes to implement the intermediate destination displays and six TextPanes to implement the remaining variable displays. In the interests of under-stand- ability, we will also use nine DrawPanes to show the various labels on the form, as opposed to more complex techniques involving display region intersections.

Examining the window, we can see that it isn't the kind we need to allow the user to resize because it's effectively an electronic version of a paper form and is already organized to show all the data in a con-strained space. We will now define the skeleton of the Freight view, which will be generated by the view method in the freight class.

Figure 4-1: A view of the freight object window.

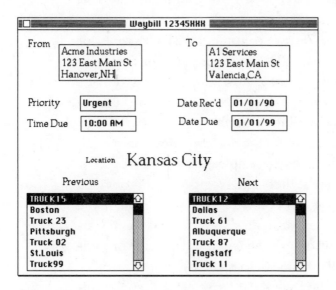

In constructing the view, we will not create a special freight pane, because we don't expect the freight view to be displayed as a sub-component of a larger, more complex view. When implementing any screen display, consider whether you are constructing something that's always found within its own special window, or is more properly a subsection of a larger display. If what you are constructing is of general use, either as a system class such as a new kind of text display, or of general use within an application such as a generalized address editor, then you should create a subclass of the Pane class.

In creating a method to display a view of a freight object, we must satisfy two specific subgoals. The first is the construction and display of the static background of the view. This background information provides information about the view in general, and about all the background labels that are to be shown in the view. The second is the construction of the individual data entry and display areas that will be used to display such things as the addresses and destination lists.

The first things we must determine is the overall size of the view and whether or not we are going to allow the user to adjust the size. In answer to the first, careful measurement tells us that the window dimensions are approximately 76 text columns by 21 text rows, or roughly the same size as an antique VDT. As far as the second, we will not allow the user to change the size of the window, they will only be able to drag it about the display. As stated, the reason for this is simple; our carefully laid out view will look terrible at twice or half our designed size. All developers know that if one provides a user with some tool that, if misused will produce unpleasant results, the user will misuse the tool and then insist that the developer fix this obvious glaring defect in their design. At this point, it is too late to remove the "feature." Strictly speaking, when designing a view, one should always be aware of the fact of whether the view is a fixed size or variable size display. All views fall into one of these types.

Now that we have established we have a fixed size view 76 columns wide and 21 rows high, and we have also determined that we are working with character measurements (as opposed to pixel measurements), we can proceed to lay out the various elements we intend to display in the view. Referring to our original sketch and making more precise measurements, we produce a list of things we would like to display, and the text coordinates of where we would like these things displayed. Table 4-2 shows the text coordinates.

Table 4-2: Text coordinates of elements to be displayed.

Field	ColStart	RowStart	ColEnd	RowEnd
Origin	C6	R5	C35	R6
Dest	C43	R2	C71	R6
Priority	C9	R7	C25	R8
DateRec'd	C50	R7	C65	R8
TimeDue	C9	R8	C25	R10
DateDue	C50	R8	C65	R9
PrevDest	C1	R11	C37	R21
NextDest	C39	R11	C78	R21

If you have not yet used the Model/Pane/Dispatcher (MPD) in Smalltalk/V, I strongly recommend that you go through the examples in the tutorial in the Smalltalk/V book before proceeding.

Summary

In commencing the implementation of our classes, the first thing we need to do is to construct a skeleton onto which we will hang the future classes that will flesh out the system. The word skeleton has been specifically chosen, as opposed to the normally used concept of a foundation, because the classes we are implementing here are more than a flat surface for us to build our future classes on. Instead, these classes affect the development of future classes, influencing their structure and communications at the deepest level.

As I've stated before, you should make every effort to develop your classes as naturally as possible. You are primarily describing the world to the computer, you are not inventing an artificial reality for it. Even if your software has no direct analog in the outside world, you want to use a great deal of common sense in developing your classes. If you don't, especially when developing these critical core classes, you will be forced to ensure that all your other classes also deal with this unbalanced view of the world, thereby causing a great deal of needless extra work.

Even though these classes are critical to the future development of the system, there is no reason for you to feel that you must analyze the requirements for these classes in extreme detail. In prototyping, you are always going to discover new things about old classes as you progress through the design cycle, therefore you shouldn't try to completely define these core classes. Instead, you should strive to define the essentials of the classes, so you can expect that future discoveries will involve adding detail to the class, rather than inserting major structural elements that radically change the behavior of the class.

In conclusion, the core classes have a dramatic impact on future prototype work. To successfully recognize this fact, and to use it to your advantage, you shouldn't try to do absolutely everything to completely implement every requirement of the class. Instead, you should ensure that you *don't* do something that will cause you extra work in the future, and that you *do* implement the essential characteristics of the class.

- Keep the design and the prototype in sync with each other, so that each is a reflection of the other.
- When implementing a class, carefully select its superclass. Putting a new class under the wrong class can cause you much unneeded work, either to undo unwanted effects of the superclass, or to do things that another class could have done for you.
- Classes implement three basic kinds of methods. Those that perform *system maintenance* functions such as initializers, those that provide *access* and *update* capabilities, and those that implement the *class specific* methods.
- Over analyzing a problem is just as bad as under analyzing a problem.
- System initialization functions are necessary during prototyping, but make sure end users cannot get at them. You will have to create single commands that can initialize central control structures, you don't have to give the user access to them.
- Try to keep the development of your classes balanced. Don't overdevelop one class at the expense of underdeveloping another.
- If users are given a command that can be abused, they will abuse it, and then insist that the unpleasant results are your fault. In many cases this can be nipped in the bud by not giving them the command in the first place.

Exercises

1. I have only illustrated the development of a few views here. Now it's your turn to repeat this process on such things as the Customer and Warehouse views.

CHAPTER 5

Dog and Pony Shows

If you can determine exactly how much it will cost, exactly how long it will take, and exactly what the result will be, you are doing the same old thing again.

In previous chapters we began the process of specifying the freight tracking system by defining the views through which users of the system would interact, supplying information to it and retrieving information from it. Although four chapters aren't really enough to scratch the surface, it isn't due to the variety of tasks, so much as to the sheer number of windows we must implement. The individual development of the Customer, Truck, and Warehouse views has been done behind the scenes and is now going to be used in this chapter, which gives us the critical mass needed to bring up the first interface.

The decision as to exactly when to show a client the first prototype has little to do with any form of computer science. Management and business texts aside, in software development it is the point where a client's crisis in confidence in you exceeds the idiosyncratic behavior of the program. In short, the client sees their first prototype when they become more of a pain than the program. Remember, to a client, software development is a mysterious process where people do all sorts of incomprehensible things for a great deal of money and are always late. The easiest way to reassure a client and to extract information from them, is to show them what they want to see. This means your prototype better be able to dance.

The primary difference at this point of development between OOP and more traditional approaches is that traditional approaches simply do not allow for any kind of interim working version to be released, which means the client is forced to wait for the majority of the project before they can play with it. I realize that there are those who are saying, "That's not true. I can release interim versions." You can, but the production of interim working versions is a far cry from an environment like Smalltalk, where the system develops within an integrated environment, is simply a subcomponent of this environment, and always operates, to some degree or another. Traditional non-OO environments often provide fine target environments after the system has been designed, tested, and certified trouble free, but by their very nature they interfere with the initial development of a complex system. I'm not saying these environments are bad; on the contrary, there are certain ones of which I'm rather fond. But for design prototyping, *flexibility*, a *powerful language*, and *environment* are the primary issues. Attempts at order can wreak havoc in this chaos. In order to stave off any possible accusations of being an anarchist, I am not recommending the disposal of current design methods. What I am discussing is the fact that you cannot abuse these tools by trying to make them handle the chaos of prototype design and not expect them to bite back by damaging your design. How many can recall projects where the source code control system got turned off during initial development because the frequency and scope of changes were turning it into a real nag? And how many can recall the chaos later when it was discovered nobody had ever turned it back on?

I would like to remind you that this is a book about prototype development, which is inherently a messy process. My recommendations are confined strictly to this domain. Anyone who would make this kind of environment available in the maintenance cycle would set loose the devil.

Our objective is to get a prototype accepted by the user. At that point, as our prototype is an executable Smalltalk program, there is no argument with its ability to accurately represent itself. This prototype is delivered to the more sterile maintenance environment which, while preventing wild new growth in capabilities, also prevents spontaneous degradation into a bug-riddled nightmare. Figure 5-1 represents this transition.

Figure 5-1: Prototype development.

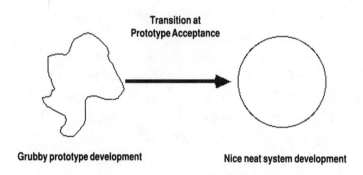

Development Review

We now are in possession of a Freight view that we have spent the last few chapters identifying and designing. In this section I will also be reintroducing the views we defined to operate with the Freight view, such as the Customer and Warehouse views. I have not included a treatise on their development in this book for the simple reason that had I done so you would now be reading Chapter 20 instead of Chapter 5. If you did not do them as exercises for the last chapter, then you may wish to hum along in a few places.

The new views are designed to complement the Freight view we have designed so we can present a system to Mr. Schroeder that at least pretends to be what we will finally deliver. The issue of "pretense" in OOP design is very important, and can be seen most clearly when systems that incorporate complex user interfaces are being constructed, although it applies equally to all design and development projects.

Faking It

In a system like this, the user interface is definitely our primary focus because it is what we are going to use to help us develop the underlying system. It could be said that the underlying system is actually nothing more than a bag of tricks that makes the interface behave the way we want it to. Admittedly, this is an extreme statement and should be taken with a grain of salt. However, it is unquestionably true that the user interface will provide us with all the information about the responsibilities of the underlying system. The user interface doesn't actually do anything other than show data to users, allow them to fiddle with some of it, and successfully recognize when users are trying to get the system to perform some specific task, such as updating the location of a piece of freight. As far as where this data comes from or how it is obtained in the first place or even what should be done with it, the user interface simply assumes this is all the responsibility of the underlying system and will be solved without bothering the interface. As I've said before, the view is a window into the underlying system. You can no more expect the view to understand the underlying system than you can expect a windowpane to understand the world you see through it.

In this case, we simply can't build the underlying system before we construct the interface, because we are depending on the interface to tell us how the underlying system behaves. We have the windows, but it may be necessary to paint scenery on them initially because they look out into a gray void. At the same time, these windows are what we will use to order this void.

This is where "pretense" enters, insofar as we intend on presenting the interfaces on the screen, even though they cannot operate because there isn't any system underneath them. In many systems, developers will attempt to accomplish this same goal by *stubbing* code, which has the machine return a response indicating that it would have performed a specific action, had the code to do it been available. In short, if you want to test the integration of a square root function into your system, but you don't have one handy and really don't need the result anyway, you could stub out the square root function as

```
function squareRoot(aNumber)
    print "if only I could compute sqrt(number)"
end
```

As an old mentor of mine used to say, "Not everything worth doing is worth doing well." I would extend that reasoning to say that in initial software prototyping, some things are not worth doing at all. If you can't display or access the data, why bother with it?

Having rationalized the lack of functionality in our user interface, we will now concentrate on what it does provide. In simple terms, we will be able to present a series of windows where we have stubbed out a few basic functions of the underlying system, so that we can provide some meaningful data in each window, making it look as if these windows are actually looking at the underlying system. In reality we have just painted a scene on each window. Our objective here is to sit our clients in front of these windows and use them in any way we can to produce responses from our client. We will be equally interested in positive and negative responses, and even more interested in any observations about information missing from any of the views. From this our client will walk away happy and we will know what changes we need to make in our design to ring their bells the next time. Given the rapid turnaround time in an integrated environment like Smalltalk, some care must be exercised so this process doesn't get out of hand and lead to more noise than action. It is probably best to let the client play with your design once a week. They will feel involved and you will get handy feedback.

Preparing for the Client

The interesting thing about doing client presentations is that they force you to stop and take a look around for a moment, in order to gather the elements of the system into some semblance of order, rehearse them a little, and then parade them by the client.

The root of the problem with many software design and development systems is that what is good for people is not good for computers, and vice versa. People are more comfortable dealing with a program as a series of chunks which are each easily understood and which have a limited number of relationships with other chunks in the program. We are most comfortable dealing with a program by decomposing it into its elemental parts.

Unfortunately, the more complex the program, the more difficult it is to deal with strictly by decomposition. OO systems solve one basic problem by providing a cohesive framework for decomposing tasks and allowing those tasks to be discussed at many different conceptual levels. In Smalltalk, there is a class for managing dictionaries, naturally called "Dictionary." All OOP systems deal with objects in context, meaning that the system always takes some external contextual factor into account, which has the capacity to affect the object itself. This means that we can talk about a Dictionary object in the context of being a Dictionary object. On the other hand, we can talk about a Dictionary object in terms of being just an object, which means we are talking about the things that are common between dictionaries and every other object under the sun. By allowing us to decompose our problems into hierarchical structures, as in "A Dictionary is a kind of Collection is a kind of Object" and then to freely mix and match our contextual references to these objects, we manage to undo much of the rat's nest created in the attempts to directly provide access to every level of the system that required them. Now we inherit this stuff and we no longer have to directly worry about it. Before inheritance, global variables and function parameters were the only two mechanisms to provide access to data between distinct program elements. By providing another mechanism and making the process implicit, this makes the job of creating and integrating elements of the system much easier. As you will find at the end of this book, this process is so easy it comes back to bother us a little in the end because the application is attached like a leech to the Smalltalk platform.

The Prototype Model

In looking up from the latest system that is making blots on our display, we should always be able to form some mental model of the system we are trying to build, beyond the listings and notes and Sanskrit-covered whiteboard. This model is simply an imaginary computer running our imaginary system. The program we are building in real life is only a copy of this imaginary program, albeit somewhat modified because of mundane and trivial details not considered in the imaginary model. This model is quite important to us, as it is the only copy of the system we can always find (and it always runs).

In consulting our model, we have an interface that consists of a group of screens, each screen displaying a particular chunk of meaningful information from the client's point of view. These chunks are all sharing a common pool of data; for example, the From address in the Freight view corresponds to the address given for the one example shipper. The screens are listed in Table 5-1.

Table 5-1: Screens from our model system.

View	Freight View Data
Freight	The starting view
Customer	Freight:(Shipper Receiver)
Warehouse	Freight:(Location,PreviousDestinations,NextDestinations)
Truck	Freight:(Location,PreviousDestinations,NextDestinations)

The views provide us with the fields shown in Table 5-2.

Table 5-2: The fields made from our views.

Freight	Customer	Warehouse	Truck
Waybill# *2*	CustomerID *Jones*	freightStored *Waybill 2*	id *Truck1* onboardFreight *Waybill3*
Origin *123 Main St.* *Boston MA*	CustomerAddress *123 Main St.* *Boston MA*	trucks *Truck3*	route *Boston*
Destination *456 Easy St.* *LA, CA*	History *Waybill1*	inbound *Truck2*	capacity *10,10,10*
Location *Denver*	InTransit *Waybill2*	outbound *Truck1*	usedCapacity *5,5,5*
Next Intermediate Destinations *Truck2* *LA* *Truck5*		capacity *100,100,100*	
Prev Intermediate Destinations *Truck1* *Boston* *Truck4*		usedCapacity *10,10,10* name *Denver*	
Customer *Jones*			
Priority *Normal*			
Date Received *<autoset>*			
Date Due *01/10/91*			
Time Due *09:00 AM*			
Dimensions *1,1,1*			

In examining our views and the data we intend to stuff into them, as if the data came from a real system underneath, we find that we need to provide navigation controls between the four views. In doing this, we allow the client to get a feel for exactly how the system behaves, in terms of the presentation of the major data elements and navigation between them. In conclusion, we have decided that there are four views we can demonstrate, which show four of the central data elements within the system. We have defined the fixed data that will be presented in each of these views, and we will implement navigation between the related elements of these four views.

Logistical details involved in management demos, affectionately known as "dog and pony shows," strongly suggest we automate our demonstration as much as possible. We know that once we get any one of these windows up on the screen, we want our system to do nothing but switch from view to view as dictated by the user. If we could, we would enter a loop so tight the only options would be switching to a connected view or resetting the system. The issue is simple, there is a correlation between the importance of a demonstration and the number of unique keys hit by a user that causes something horrible to happen. In short, if the demo is very important, and there is only one 60-character string that will crash the program, rest assured that will be the first thing the user types. Some users have a particularly malicious attitude towards new software. One very wise man refused to accept software until it didn't crash when he a) sat on the keyboard, and b) ran his elbows up and down the keyboard until a few of the caps popped off. When entering any "demo" situation, limit the possibilities as much as possible. Don't kid yourself or your clients into thinking that this software is operational. Until the system is truly operational, keep your demo interface locked down tight. Remember, a primary unspoken function of a demo is to reenforce your clients' confidence in you. Therefore, you should always take steps to rig the situation accordingly.

Reviewing our immediate objectives one final time, we must:

- Bind the demo initialization data to the four views we will show
- Test each of the views
- Link the views together in a navigation path
- Implement a "quick start" command to bring up and lock in the demo
- Make a handout package that illustrates each of the views
- Look presentable

Preparing for the Demonstration

In preparing to demonstrate our prototype to the client, we are performing a task that isn't *directly* involved in the creation of the new system. We are doing this to reassure the client, because if we don't, we might not have the opportunity to keep working on the task. Since this is critical to the future success of the system, we do want to do a good job. On the other hand, since this doesn't represent work we will necessarily deliver in the final prototype, we don't want to do too good of a job.

This is a delicate balancing act, one that you will become more comfortable with as you gain experience in the RP environment. For now, you want to concentrate your efforts in areas where you get the biggest payoff for the least amount of work, since you can't assume that the time you invest in building the demonstration prototype will be of much use in anything but the prototype.

Painting the Scenery

In binding the initialization data to each of the views, we are admittedly producing code we will simply discard later as the real system is constructed and integrated with the views.

To bind the data to the Freight view, we must first identify the points at which the freight view looks for this data. At this point in the system's evolution, it is a simple process; we need only locate the name message for each of the subpanes. All individual panes within the system expect their model to provide a simple message that allows the pane to obtain the data it should display. For text panes, this is usually the name message or a variant, and the pane expects to receive a String object. For graphics panes, this is usually the *form:* message, and the pane expects to receive a bitmap in response to this message.

In our case, we don't have to deal with graphics yet, so we simply need to implement the various methods the panes will need and make each one return the appropriate text string. As the system evolves, we will be replacing these hardwired strings with more complex logic that produces real values from the underlying system.

Reviewing the view method in the Freight class, we find that there are nine separate panes within the view and each of them specifies a unique name method. In reexamining the other methods in the Freight class, we find that each of the name methods has already been implemented, each returning the similarly named instance variable of a Freight object. Given the way views are defined, it isn't too surprising to find a tight relationship between elements of the view (panes) and elements of the model object (instance variables). This is not true forever since, as the system evolves, the relations between instance variables and panes becomes far more complex and problematical. At the start, however, most instance variables and panes within views are linked on a one-to-one basis.

As all of the subpanes display data from instance variables, all we need to do is stuff our test values into these instance variables when each instance of the Freight class is created. We've already created one such method, the *origin:destination:location:customer:dateDue:timeDue:prev: next:* message, which is the first cut at a standard freight object construction function. I call this a construction function rather than an initialization function because its goal is not so much the raw initialization of the object as it is the insertion of initial data into this object from external sources.

After all is said and done, the only new code we need to implement is something that configures the Freight object by sending the constructor message given above in conjunction with the desired parameters. Here is the code used to accomplish this:

```
demo
  ^self origin: '123 Main St.
     Boston MA'
     destination: '456 Easy St.
     LA, CA'
     location: 'Denver'
     customer: 'Jones'
     dateDue: '01/10/91'
     timeDue: '09:00 AM'
     prev: #('Truck1' 'Boston' 'Truck4')
     next: #('Truck2' 'LA' 'Truck5')
```

With the demo instance method in the Freight class, we can now produce a Freight object with a known, valid configuration on demand through the following message sequence:

```
newFreightObject := Freight new demo.
```

Testing Each View

Now that we can easily produce a properly initialized freight object, producing the view isn't much more difficult. The message sequence *Freight new demo view* will produce the view on the screen every time we call it. Because we were forced to do a lot of testing in our initial attempt to present the view in Chapter 4, our testing now focuses on more client-specific issues. In this case, we know the basic view is OK, so we are left deciding if we should address some of the cosmetic issues we previously postponed. Recall that we drew a pretty picture of the original Freight view, with features ranging from mundane details like labels for each of the subpanes to fancier things like having the location displayed in a larger font.

The way we decide on final alterations to the view is similar to the way we originally decided not to do these tasks. Previously, when we were creating the view, we were concerned with the mechanics of the view itself, in terms of the distinct panes that form the view and the object(s) from which the view data is obtained. Background labels and fancy display options didn't have any direct relationship with these criteria, so we ignored them. Now the criteria have changed. Instead of focusing on the technical details of implementing the view, we are concerned with the client's perception of the view. To them fancy fonts in the first prototype are going to seem a complete waste of time. Background labels, on the other hand, are not optional. Therefore, in testing each view in terms of its *estimated* acceptability to the client, we realize we must now add background labels to the pane.

Given Smalltalk's focus on the composition of views from sub-views, we might expect to implement the labels as a series of text panes of some type, each preloaded with one of the labels. But this would be a great deal of typing, to add nine new panes to the Freight view just so we can have labels. Since we have fixed the size of the Freight view and don't have to worry about the user resizing it, we can solve this problem more simply.

Smalltalk does not prevent you from defining panes that overlap within a view. In fact, as you are about to see, you can exploit this to your advantage. By defining a new pane that covers the entire area of the view, we have a single pane in which we can place all of our labels. In fact, by using the DrawPane class, we can simply dump the labels right onto the window, bypassing the panes entirely.

Briefly, the DrawPane class sets the drawing environment to the current window and then calls the showWindow function in the model given for the pane. To produce the view with labels, we simply add a Draw pane to the view method code and provide a showWindow method for it to use. The DrawPane creation sequence inserted into the view method would be

```
aTopPane addSubpane:
    (DrawPane new model: self;
        framingRatio: (0 @ 0 extent: (1 @ 1))).
and the new showWindow method would be;
```

```
showWindow
  'FROM' displayAt: 5 @ 60.
  'TO' displayAt: 380 @ 60.
 'PRIORITY' displayAt: 10 @ 200.
 'RECD' displayAt: 410 @ 200.
 'DLVR TIME' displayAt: 5 @ 220.
 'DLVR DATE' displayAt: 410 @ 220.
 'LOCATION' displayAt: 320 @ 257.
 'PREVIOUS LOCATIONS' displayAt: 50 @ 285.
 'FUTURE LOCATIONS' displayAt: 520 @ 285.
```

In order to make this technique work in the general case, the existing DrawDispatcher class has been modified to always return False in response to isControlWanted. I find this to be useful; usually I use subclasses of the ScrollDispatcher to implement anything that actually interacts with the user. If you choose not to override the behavior of isControlWanted in the DrawDispatcher class, you won't be able to use the above technique without modification

Navigation

To implement navigation between the panes, we must first review the views we will be presenting and determine exactly what the links are between them. Doing this, we come up with the relationships shown in Table 5-3.

Table 5-3: Relationships between the panes.

StartView	StartPane	EndView
Freight	From	Customer
Freight	Previous	Truck
Freight	Next	Truck
Freight	Location	Warehouse
Warehouse	FreightStored	Freight
Warehouse	Trucks	Truck
Warehouse	TrucksArriving	Truck
Warehouse	TrucksLeaving	Truck
Truck	Route	Warehouse
Truck	Freight	Freight
Customer	Order	Freight

As architects of the original system we will make an arbitrary and capricious decision that, for the time being, a mouse click within a pane indicates the user's desire to have a new window created showing the linked data. If we click on the Freight data pane From, we want the system to create a new Customer view and display it on the screen.

This is extremely easy in the case of any ListPanes in the views, such as the previous and next destination lists in the freight view. The ListPane class implements a "change" behavior that will allow us to know whenever the user clicks in a list pane. The logic behind it is simple, the primary job of a list box is to allow users to select items from a list and no matter where you click in a list box, you are clicking on an item in the list. ListPanes accept change: messages, the parameters of which are the messages the ListPane should return to the model whenever the user attempts to change their selection by clicking on a different item in the list. If you examine the code in the Freight class, you will find that the next and previous destination list panes both define a change: message. Looking further, you will find both of these methods implemented in the Freight class. If you examine the methods themselves, you will see I have already passed through here, as each method does nothing but create a Truck view and transfer control to it.

Demo Package

The demo package consists of the demo software itself, a handout to be given to the client, and a script that you will follow when performing the demo. The script is for your own use, the handout is to be left with the client, and you can use your own judgement in deciding whether or not to leave the demo software with the client.

Handout

An actual physical handout may seem like an inconsequential detail, but I can assure you, it isn't! The function of a client walkthrough is always twofold: to extract new information from the client and to re-assure the client that you haven't fallen off a cliff. In order to accom-plish this, we undeniably "rig" demos, making things seem to do far more than they actually do. We do this with only positive intentions, but we must ensure that it doesn't backfire on us. The more successful our demo, the more we will need our handouts to defend us.

The problem is simple, it deals with the client's natural reactions after the demo has come and gone. The simple fact of the matter is that the client's reasoning processes appear to possess mass, continu-ing along in the directions started by the demo for several days. On one hand, if the demo was a failure, in a few days you may hear from them that your services are no longer required. Conversely, if your demo was a success, the client's rapidly increasing opinion of the system's capabilities may doom your next demo.

By leaving the client with a handout package that shows each of the screens they saw, and clearly details what was real and what wasn't, you prevent this common runaway reaction. The handout provides the anchor when you aren't around, keeping the client from gaining or losing too much faith in you.

Last Survey

Now that you're finished, take one last look around, brush the crumbs off your shirt and make a solemn promise never to spill a Coke on the keyboard again. Then go out, find someone who's opinion you re-spect, and briefly run your demo by them. Their reaction will help you anticipate the client's reactions in certain areas, and it gives you a chance to polish your presentation. I realize that you may feel that you are a programmer and this has nothing to do with you, but if you are in any way involved in the development of "new" software, you should pay attention. Because software development is both expen-sive and risky, it behooves you to give your clients a warm fuzzy once in a while, to avoid a cold brush off in the future. By showing them the software as it evolves, in terms they can understand, you will do much to gain their support. By rigorously controlling the setting, as we have done in orchestrating the demo, we do the most we can to guarantee a successful outcome.

So run through the system a few more times, checking to make sure all the right data is showing up in the windows. Try the borderline conditions to make sure it's not going to crash if you try something a little different in the demonstration. Where you have unavoidable weak spots, work up some kind of misdirection so that they won't be noticed.

Finally, you need to build the release kit. The situation you confront when doing this can vary greatly, from the client arriving to see the software run on the development machine, to the software being taken to the client's site and loaded onto a machine that isn't even the same species as the development machine. In the first case it might seem that a release kit is unnecessary, and in the second that it would be impossible to assemble one. Both assumptions are incorrect.

In the first case, you should always make a release kit at times like these, because it gives you a fixed point in time to return to should you meet some future calamity. In the second case, Smalltalk as a language is remarkably consistent across platforms, allowing source to be moved from an IBM-PC and run on a Macintosh or Sun computer, unchanged. But whatever the case, make two copies of the release kit, use one when you need it and keep the other one handy, hoping you never do need that one. But don't neglect the creation of the release kit, because the history of a project's most vivid portrayal will be in the increasing sophistication of the releases over time.

Summary

While the client demonstrations may not seem to be an integral process of software development, I hope that you realize their importance in the overall scheme of things. In software development, especially in situations when you are prototyping new, vaguely defined software, you need to make special efforts to ensure that the client is involved in the process and can see that steady progress is being made.

In doing this, you are going to have to make the software pretend to be something that it isn't, to one extent or another. There are two kinds of pretense, one good and one bad. In the first case, as illustrated in this chapter, you are simply adding code that gives an idea of how the finished system will behave. In other words, what you are showing is how the final system would act, if only it had the code it needed to act this way. The latter case is better described as fraud, when you make the software behave in a way that you have no intentions of actually supporting. In short, it's OK to make software seem to be something it's not for a demo, providing that you do mention that the software is doing this, and that you really do intend on making the software actually behave this way.

- Some demonstrations are often driven by a client's anxiety level, and are primarily meant to reduce this level.
- Demonstrations are a valuable source of information, because the client can tell you a lot more about their desires when they see something physical that reflects what you believe their desires are.
- The system doesn't have to be completely operational to demonstrate it.
- You can hardwire data into systems where the real data management functions do not yet exist.
- Rehearse your demonstration before seeing the client. Make sure you stick to a script as much as possible, and try to avoid known problem areas.
- Leave the client with a handout that clearly indicates what was real and what was faked.

Exercises

1. Our client is considering this software for over 500 PCs and is not amused by our allowing the user to open many views at once. We don't want him to start figuring the cost of our contract against the 500 meg of RAM he feels we are forcing him to buy. Quickly modify the design so that only one window is open at a time.
2. Your demo crashes in an unexpected way in front of the client. What do you do?

CHAPTER 6

Behind the Windows

A lot of what appears to be progress is just so much technological rococo.

Having finished our dog and pony show with Mr. Schroeder, we have received both his blessing on the initial interface and a swift kick indicating we should make the interface more operational, post haste.

As I noted earlier, pretense is a big issue in rapid prototyping, as the proper use of it can save you a great deal of unnecessary work. Unfortunately, as the primary source of your feedback is your client, there is very little you can do to truly hide the fact that a large portion of the "software" is a fake. The more sophisticated your presentation, the more the client will attempt to truly "use" the system, which in turn will cause the system's pretenses to become more visible. If you have done a good job making the windows look like they are connected to a running system, the user is going to attempt to use them as though they were. The bottom line is that the user is going to attempt to enter data into these windows, which is something they cannot do. Although the previous demonstration was essentially an acceptance test for the master interface windows, the true definition of success is not the client's approval of the windows, it's their demand that you make the windows work, so that they can enter data into them. In other words, your job is to make the demo look real. In return, if you are successful, the client will realize it is not real and complain about it.

So, here we are. Our demonstration was a complete success, and Mr. Schroeder is eagerly awaiting the next installation and next time, he's going to poke at it a lot harder. To do this, we need to "activate" the fields we have already placed in the windows. In Chapter 5, we actually implemented a number of the service methods supporting data display in the views, but we simply bound the functions directly to string values, effectively hardwiring these values into the system. Now we must return to these methods and begin to tie them to real underlying data.

Enhancing the Views

In enhancing the views, we will be concentrating on making them "real." When we demonstrated the prototype we had, for the most part, worked out what a view looked like, but we had hardwired both its data and its behavior. Now it is time for us to actually add logic to the system in order to make the view more intelligent, so that it can extract the necessary data from the underlying model and can intelligently react to user actions within the view.

Reevaluating the Design

In order to determine what we should do next, we must first reexamine where we are. This is not some trivial observation, but is one of the great dividing issues between RP design and more traditional methods. In traditional methods, a single, albeit long, pass is made through the system, carefully defining it at every step of the way. When this task is finished, the design is done and ready to be coded, or at least that's how the argument goes.

In RP design, we stop designing on a regular basis in order to run the prototype by the clients and users, thereby getting information on adjusting our design before it's too late to do anything about the parts they hate, or the things they really wish it had. So, for all my arguments about seamless development environments, it appears that our design actually progresses by fits and starts, as opposed to the seamless path of traditional design evolution.

As it happens, this observation is wrong. These sessions with the client are not "seams" in the RP design process, they are natural components of it. They provide us with the means to continually adjust our design course and goals as we learn more about what the client desires by letting them interact with our best idea of what it is that they do desire. As they do this, they will provide us with the necessary information to extend the design another level. Recall that I observed at the outset of this book that it wasn't realistic to expect to get a clear list of requirements from a client when you commence a design project. We are designing to the requirement we have and then using that design to dig up more requirement information.

For this reason, it is important to reevaluate your design position after each session with the client. If you feel that because the client didn't have a fit when they saw the prototype there isn't any reason to perform this reevaluation, you haven't yet noticed that we don't have a real clear idea of what we are supposed to do next. Yes, we know that we need to keep going forward, moving from a rough prototype to a finished product. That knowledge is of little use in creating the freight management system. Only by reevaluating our current position in terms of what we have learned from the client can we determine exactly what it is we should do next. So, as you see, this reevaluation is far from a trivial detail, it is the central driving force in an RP project.

The first step in reevaluating the design is to sit down with the prototype and make notes about its current capabilities and those capabilities we would like it to have next. After playing with the Freight view for a while, we come away with the following observations:

- We can already alter text in any of the fields. If we try to save the text the system complains.
- We can click on an element in the previous or future location lists and the system responds by telling us it doesn't know how to handle these kinds of selections.
- We have to do something about the way the view is loaded with data, as in acquiring real data from a real freight object.
- Existing navigation tools are already fine, we just need to make sure they work with real data as well as they do with the demo data.

Now that we have determined some of the existing characteristics of the system, we need to determine what we want its future characteristics to be. We know that, in general, we want to make the interface more sophisticated. Given the behavior of our interface now, the best path for us to follow is to truly integrate the views with the objects they are displaying. This will allow us to present a prototype that can create, access, and manage these objects through the views.

In determining how to implement what appears to be a database of the various objects which our new improved views will be capable of displaying, we know we don't want to spend too much time actually implementing the database logic, if for no other reason than Schroeder trucking already has a nice corporate database system. We can integrate the final freight management system with their existing database. Therefore, we'd like to waste as little time in this area as possible. We know immediately that one of the largest "pretenders" in the new system will be the underlying database system.

Given these considerations about the database aspects of the interface, we can say that our objective is to present the same views as we did the last time, but allow the information in the views to be edited, saved, and retrieved by the user.

Upgrading the Prototype

The first step in upgrading the prototype is to carefully examine the object behind the view and ensure that it possesses the necessary capabilities to support more sophisticated view operations. Where we now have fixed strings wired into the system, we will need to implement complete two-way communications between the view and the object being viewed.

Examining the existing code, we find that after the freight object is initialized, it is sent a demo message, which forces the demonstration data into the object. Our first task is to examine the actions of the demo initialization method and determine if we need to move any of this logic to the freight view.

Examining these two methods, we don't find anything in the demo method that needs to be moved to the initialize method, but we do find one thing that could stand to be changed in the initialization method. Where we now place a nil value in the freight object's dateReceived field, we should really put today's date. After all, if a new Freight object is being created, the odds are pretty good that it was received today. If it wasn't, they can always change the date in the view.

Accomplishing this is not too difficult, we simply replace the statement:

```
dateReceived := nil.
```

with

```
dateReceived := Date today.
```

in the initialize method.

Continuing along, we check the behavior of the Freight view when we don't load the demo data. In short, where we originally brought up a Freight view with the command:

```
Freight new demo view
```

we now wish to skip the demo initialization sequence. When we do this, after having updated the initialization method to set today's date into the dateReceived field, we are rewarded with a view where all the display values are empty except for the dateReceived display, which shows today's date.

This examination of the system and alteration of the initialization code is the first part of the two-part enhancement operation. Before you can actually begin enhancing the performance of the system, you must first examine its current behavior. Obviously, the existing system must be reviewed before any detailed plans are formed concerning its enhancement. In doing this we are not simply determining the foundation upon which we will be building, we are also removing elements that will conflict with this future development. Before you proceed, you must first remove any obvious impediments to progress. This isn't to say you will find them all; you won't, but you will trip over them later. The sooner you find and correct these little imperfections in your design, the easier that correction will be. As the software grows, changing elements that have a wide influence can be a difficult and painful exercise. While OOPD is an extremely efficient way of developing complex software, it is not a panacea. Many things that are painful in conventional design environments are equally painful in OO environments.

The first thing to do is to allow the user to enter text into the panes. The basic capabilities of the text panes we have used in the view already allow the user to enter text into the fields in the view, and the basic editing functions such as backspacing and cut and paste operations are also implemented by these panes. Our problem is not how to allow the user to enter text into the fields in the view, it is recognizing when they have done so and deciding exactly what we intend to do about it.

The first step is to cease using the demo method to load the Freight view with data by force. We will keep the demo method around for a while longer, as it may be useful as a test method in the future, should we unknowingly damage the system. Dropping the demo method is not very hard, we just bring up a new Freight view with

```
Freight new view
```

leaving the demo message off the end of the message sequence. If you try this right now, you will be rewarded with a completely empty Freight view, save for the legends and the outlines around each data entry field. If you attempt to move around the screen and enter text, you will find that you can click the mouse and then enter text into any one of the text panes, but the two list panes at the bottom seem to ignore you, or possibly trigger comments about saving changes if you have entered text into any of the text fields. The comments indicate that each individual text field must be aware of whether or not it has been changed, although this doesn't appear to be a major issue when simply moving between text fields. If, on the other hand, you move to either a List pane (the previous and future destination lists) or you attempt to close the Freight view, you will be presented with a dialog box asking if you wish to save or discard your changes.

In the interest of simplicity, I am not going to deal directly with the logic behind this behavior, but instead will address all those things that we have not yet implemented for the various panes within the Freight view. In short, the entire save/cancel logic is closely intertwined with the methods we link to the panes to support user operations such as selecting, saving, and deleting.

Plug-In Methods

Before dealing with the specifics of the Freight view, we must first deal with the general concept of "plug-in" methods. This concept allows us to create and use general purpose classes such as list and text editing panes, and to easily customize their behavior in individual applications *without requiring us to generate a new subclass*. In many cases, specific application classes are derived from existing system classes so the application class simply has to modify the general behavior of the system class in order to achieve the results it wants.

The most common example of this is the constant subclassing of the object class and pane classes. In the first case, it is unlikely that a standard Smalltalk distribution package is already going to contain the classes we need for our application and many of these new classes are only related to the rest of the hierarchy insofar as they are all subclasses of the Object class. The Freight class we are now implementing is an excellent example of this case.

Whenever we need to implement a special kind of display field, we will implement it as a class of Subpane. For example, in future work, we may end up with a good many views that display a customer's address and a few other tidbits about them. If we find ourselves using this in many different views, we could implement the CustomerPane class as a subclass of the TextPane class, thereby allowing us simply to add a CustomerPane to our views, using the customer object itself as a model. In short, if you use the existing classes, such as TextPane, you must provide detailed logic on the data path between your specialized application object and the more general behavior of the existing class. A TextPane knows nothing about customer objects, it understands only text. Everywhere you use a TextPane to show information on a customer, you must provide logic to extract data from the customer and present it to the text pane in a palatable form. If you find yourself doing this often, you would be advised to create the CustomerPane class under TextPane and move the logic there. Then the logic is automatically available to all users of the CustomerPane, which will keep the overall size and complexity of your code down.

Unfortunately, there is one major problem with this approach. If each level must be overridden to do application-specific work, we could easily end up with hundreds of subclasses under the TextPane, with most of these subclasses implementing trivial operations. In certain circumstances, we could end up with a real mess on our hands as we implement dozens of application-specific subclasses of the Text-Pane class. Consider if we simply provided a "Notes" editor, which allowed the user to attach a piece of text to any of the major objects such as customers and freight shipments. Does this mean that we have to implement a subclass of TextPane for every different kind of note we intend on saving?

Fortunately for us, the answer is no because of the plug-in concept. The idea behind plug-in methods is that classes should directly implement only that behavior which is known to be common in all cases. In the case of a TextPane, it doesn't really matter what you are using the pane for, it is going to perform certain basic tasks like inserting and deleting characters the same way. Other tasks however, are unlikely to be done the same way twice. Which is where the plug-in methods enter the picture.

Plug-in methods are most heavily used in the various subclasses of the Subpane class, such as text and list panes. We are already experienced with the fact that we don't need to create a new pane class for every kind of object we intend on displaying, we simply provide an instance of that class as the model for the new pane, and expect the pane to be intelligent enough to get its data from that pane. Unfortunately, this alone still requires that we use models closely related to each other in the hierarchy so the pane knows how to deal with the data we have provided it. In other words, we can give a list pane any list as a model, or a text pane any text as a model, but we cannot give a list to a text pane or vice versa. Although this might appear to be an unreasonable goal, it prevents us from providing the same Customer object to both a text and a list pane and expecting the text pane to automatically show the address of the customer and the list pane to automatically show the customer's freight shipments.

Consider when we tell a text pane that it is to save the new data we have entered into it. Exactly what should this mean to the pane?

From TextPane's point of view, it means that the data displayed is correct and it should forget about the fact that we edited the data. But to the model, the saving of the data is a far more personal event and is very specific to the model being used. A Customer might react by updating the customer's address or shipping history, depending on what kind of data was displayed in the pane that is performing the save operation.

In this specific case, the TextPane will attempt to inform its model about the change. Since it doesn't know beforehand exactly how the model updates itself, it expects the creator of the text pane to plug in the name of the message that should be send to the model. This parameter is provided through the change: message, sent to a TextPane when it is created. When the TextPane attempts to save its current contents, it will send the supplied change message to its model, with the text as a parameter, so the model knows what the new text is. This means that the text pane can deal with what it knows to be unchangeable facts, such as successful saves to clear the dirty flag in the text pane, and will allow the model to implement the behaviors it isn't too sure about.

The end result of all this is that a partnership is formed between the generalized capabilities of the TextPane and the application-specific capabilities of the model, be it a Customer or anything else. The TextPane expects its creator to provide information about what it should say to the model when certain things happen, which means that the TextPane only needs to know when to send a message, it doesn't care what the message is or what the end result of sending that message will be. All TextPanes know that the supplied change message should be sent to their models when the user tries to save the text in the pane, but they are oblivious to what happens after that.

If we enter an address into the Freight view at this point, we are rewarded with an error window from Smalltalk—see Figure 6-1.

As you can see, the gist of this error message is that the Freight object doesn't understand the change message, in this case the origin:from: message. Digging deeper into the code by activating the debugger, we find that it was the accept method in the TextPane class that got the change message and sent it to the Freight object and the two parameters it sent along with the message were the text that had been entered into the pane and the Dispatcher that is managing this text pane.

Figure 6-1: Smalltalk's error window.

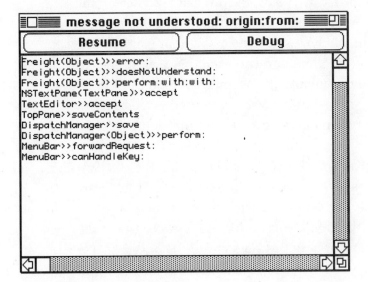

Incorporating the Plug-Ins

Returning to the specifics of the freight management system, we now see that our immediate task is to finish linking the plug-in methods to the panes and finish creating these methods within the Freight class to prevent future complaints about unknown messages. After this, we can expect the Freight view to load the various text panes with data from the Freight object that serves as the model, using the plug-in methods we have specified. When we have accomplished this for all views, we will be ready to return to Mr. Schroeder with a new software model that contains more functionality than its predecessor.

Plug-ins are, as a concept, found in almost all class hierarchies implementing window displays, but there is no accepted standard for exactly how they behave, in terms of the messages that are exchanged between the generic and application sections. There are, however, certain observations that apply to all plug-in mechanisms.

The most important detail, towering over all other considerations is that plug-ins were not provided as either a marketing gimmick or strictly as a service to you, the end user of the class hierarchy. Instead, they were implemented primarily to save the original designers of the class hierarchy a great deal of time and effort. In Smalltalk, the main function of the class hierarchy as a whole is to implement the Smalltalk development environment, a consideration that applies to at least 70 percent of the code you will encounter. This applies without question to the plug-in facilities, as they are used extensively to support all of those fancy windows you can call up with one command or another.

Given that this is the case, the best way to learn about the mechanics of the plug-in classes is to examine a class such as the ClassHierarchyBrowser which implements a window containing a set of panes used to navigate through the class hierarchy and inspect the code it contains. By looking at how this class creates its panes, how it communicates with the underlying Smalltalk class dictionary, and through extensive use of the debugger, you can watch this class establish the connections between the general purpose panes such as the list displays and text editors and the underlying data the pane is operating on, in this case the raw source code of the class hierarchy itself.

It isn't necessary for you to understand the details of these connections between the model and the generic panes. All you really need to do is identify the basic sequence used to set up the relationship in an existing class such as the class hierarchy browser, copy this list of messages into your new window construction method, and try and get the window up on the screen. As the system exercises the various plug-in functions, you will receive various debugging messages informing you that one message or another wasn't understood. Using the debugging information to determine the context in which the system is using this message, you can make a decision to either implement some supporting method in your model, or to simply drop that section of the plug-in logic in some cases. Finally, your window will appear on the screen. When this happens you should attempt to interact with it, this will produce another horde of debugging messages, indicating new plug-in relationships that need to be satisfied. You can either implement these functions now, or publish a short list of advice telling users about your unsupported features. In short, you must provide the necessary plug-in logic for the system to access the model and obtain the display data, but you don't have to provide the dynamic interface logic, as long as you ensure that the users understand that although it's a pretty window, nobody's home.

A Small Chicken and Egg Problem

Before concluding this chapter, I would like to bring one small detail to your attention, if you haven't already noticed it. We have cheerfully assumed, up to this point, that views such as the FreightManifest view are always opened on existing freight manifests. In fact, we have assumed that one is always in possession of an instantiated FreightManifest object before deciding it would be nice to view its contents. In the initial phases of prototyping this is an excellent decision, as it keeps us from having to worry about a lot of trivia when we are trying to determine the overall gross characteristics of the system. At this point, however, it isn't a good idea, for the simple reason that it makes absolutely no provision for the way things work in the real world.

Real-world users, as opposed to the perfect specimens we have been imagining up to now, primarily wish to do two things, neither of which we currently support. The first is that they don't usually have an instantiated FreightManifest object they suddenly decide they wish to examine; instead, they decide it would be nice to look at a freight manifest and then they decide it would be nice to pick a freight manifest to look at. While they may have a very good idea of what freight manifest they wish to look at, they don't actually have the object itself.

They know something, like its waybill number, that uniquely identifies it. Worse yet, they sometimes decide that the manifest they wish to see is not yet in the system. Therefore, they wish to create their envisioned manifest, as opposed to selecting one that is already in the system.

Given the fact that we want to show more detailed operational characteristics during the next major system demonstration, we must do something to solve this problem, effectively moving our prototype further away from the clean artificial world it was born in and closer to the messy real world it will have to live in. The solution to the problem is fairly simple and will serve you well as a practical introduction to using the plug-in functions.

The solution is to augment the view presentation mechanism, providing a facility that will execute the existing view presentation method based on the users selection of a specific object. In doing this, we have an excellent reason to implement a class method, one that is defined at the class level, rather than at the specific object level. Where we now expect the user to send a view message to an existing object, such as a Freight object, we will provide another mechanism at the class level to allow the user to select or create the object they intend on viewing. To accomplish this, we will have to ensure that our system implements the methods shown in Table 6-1 at the class level.

With these two methods, you can boil the user interface down to <class> select view. This message allows the user to select or create an object of <class> with little fuss.

Table 6-1: Methods to be implemented in our system.

Method	Purpose
enumerate	Lists all instances of this object. Examine the object class to see how this can be done, as you will find that you don't have to maintain a list in each class. If you hunt around, you will find Smalltalk already knows about every object that exists within the system, and therefore can provide you with a list of all objects in a certain class.

Method	Purpose
select	Presents the list generated by the enumerate message in a simple window containing a single list pane. Present the item 'New <...>' to this list, where you have replaced <...> with the appropriate term such as FreightManifest or Truck. If the user selects an existing object, return it. If they select the 'New' item, create a new object and return it.

Summary

So this is the thanks we get for a successful demonstration. The client likes the demonstration, attempts to use the software, and then insists we stop pretending and make it really do "something." This is the outcome of every successful demonstration.

Before actually getting on with making the software do more, you do want to ensure that the software isn't doing something the client objected to. The reason behind this is simple, if you were to extend the capabilities first, and fix the problems later, you would be giving yourself more work to do and undo. (In this case, due to the author's extremely close relationship to Mr. Schroeder, being able to read his mind as it were, there are no complaints.)

In this chapter we have seen the start of the next phase of the prototyping process. After we have verified that the overall objective is the one desired by the client, and we have determined that the surface behavior of the system—as manifested in the views—is appropriate, we can begin to flesh out the real behavior of the system. This path clearly illustrates where RP shares certain concepts with traditional design methodologies, namely that top-down design is not a bad thing, especially if the designer is moving towards a more detailed understanding of the problem.

This process of constant refinement is illustrated in the class hierarchy itself, in terms of the fact that it is a hierarchy in the first place, and that the classes supporting plug-in methods, actually require the application to further specialize their behavior. OOP is a process of constant refinement, in terms of creating new applications from scratch and modifying the behavior of existing systems. In implementing OOP systems, especially prototypes, you should recognize this fact and exploit it wherever possible.

As we descend deeper into the system, we will often encounter issues dealing with initialization. Much of the initial design of the prototype deals with what to do with data once you have it, but it doesn't pay much attention to how that data is acquired or created in the first place. There is nothing wrong with this, it's the natural way of things. You always want to concentrate first on the structure of data and its behavior before you pay attention to its origins. For this reason you also always want to be aware of the fact that, after designing the views and runtime behaviors for an object, you will most likely have to deal with issues involving where this data orifinally came from. In OO programming in general, and especially in RP, chickens usually evolve before eggs.

- The result of any successful demonstration are demands that the software do more.
- Don't do more until you are sure you aren't doing something you shouldn't.
- A great deal of directional control comes from client demos. In many cases they *do* know what you are supposed to do next, and you *don't*.
- After you have determined the layout and simulated behavior of a view is appropriate, you must begin to bolt the view to the real underlying objects that serve as its model.
- In Smalltalk, the best way to find holes in the software is to exercise the code and examine the complaints from the debugger about unknown methods.
- Complaints from the debugger about missing methods are not commands to implement these methods. These complaints can be treated as advice on areas of the system to ignore.

- Use the *plug-in* concept wherever possible. Plug-ins allow you to specialize the behavior of a class without subclassing it.
- As you disconnect hardwired data from the prototype and incorporate real processing logic, you will be forced to deal with issues involving the origin of the data.

Exercises

1. Where I have simply mentioned various plug-in methods for the freight view and what their general responsibilities are, you should implement real logic to perform the necessary actions. Make the freight view work.
2. After the freight view works to your satisfaction, do the same thing for the other views you have implemented.

CHAPTER 7

Externally Imposed Requirements

One man's red tape is another man's system.

We have now extended the facilities of the system to the point where it appears we are truly doing something with the data, though we know we really aren't. At this point, our job becomes more difficult because we are no longer able to show our progress simply by presenting new views. In the previous chapter, we implemented a set of plug-in functions for each of our views, allowing a user to enter reasonable data into the views and perform basic editing and selecting operations. Additionally, we implemented a basic database that captured the data entered in the views and thereby allowed the user to navigate between the views based on the common information between them. For example, users could select a Truck in a Freight Manifest view and would be presented with information on the truck that they had selected.

We haven't really implemented any kind of serious database here; instead, we have created a bucket into which we can dump all of the data entered by the user. When we need to locate some related data, such as information on a truck in a freight manifest, we look through this bucket and rely more on brute force than on skill to locate the information on the truck. Now that the basic view logic is satisfactory, we are going to have to examine the underlying objectives of the system and begin to produce code that implements these objectives. However, we should be selective about what we do and do not implement, as we are trying to work out new logic and concepts and not trying to prove we can do the same old thing again. In short, we can ignore requirements for such things as the computation of sales taxes, as we know that problem has been solved hundreds of times in every computer language ever designed. We need to concentrate on the necessary logic for our design that is unique to this system.

Requirements Analysis

The tasks involved here come under the general heading of requirements analysis, where the environment in which the system must operate is carefully examined to determine what constraints it places on the system. The environment is far more important than the hardware on which the software will be running; it also encompasses such things as external systems and the people the software must interact with. The essential goal is to ensure the software operates by rules that have been established over time, instead of ignoring these rules and forcing everyone to start over.

While we have done a fair amount of requirements analysis up to now, a great deal of it has been fuzzy. This is because we have been trying to determine strategic issues, issues we agreed at the outset were not clearly defined. Now having validated our strategy, we are beginning to focus on tactical issues which are definitely not fuzzy. There is little room for error in the interface between our freight management system and the corporate database as we are simply using the database, not creating it from scratch. For this reason we must analyze the current behavior of the database in order to produce a set of requirements that defines how our software will use it. Because we are being *dictated to* at this point, rather than *dictating* how things will be done, we can fall back on our traditional analysis tools to determine what to do next.

The Database Interface

In this case, the main emphasis is on the database interface and the way that the views will need to operate in order to interact with it. We cannot actually access the real database from the prototype because there is no way for the Smalltalk package to communicate with the database. The two main Smalltalk packages available for the Macintosh and PC do support external code modules, but it is beyond the scope of this book to discuss the mechanics of these interfaces. More importantly, it isn't necessary that we physically interact with the database at this point, only that we structure the logic so we know beyond a shadow of a doubt that this can be done.

We know that Schroeder Trucking uses an SQL (Structured Query Language) interface with their database, which is based on the relational database model. The SQL language is non-procedural, meaning it isn't dependant on the order in which things are done, instead it deals with everything in terms of statements and queries. If you make a statement in SQL, it causes the database to be altered so that it conforms with the statement you have made. If you make a query about the database, your query will be answered with information contained in the database. This book is certainly not a tutorial on SQL and I shall strive to keep the examples simple enough to be understood by use of common sense and experience.

Locking Down the Views

The first step in interacting with the database is to obtain some information on how it expects our application to interact with it. We know from our initial research that the basic information shown in each view corresponds to a particular table in the database. Therefore, we know that as we enter each view we will need to inform the database about the particular table we will be using so that it can make the appropriate data available to us. For now, we don't even need to know the exact name of the table, we can assume it has the same name as our view. If we open a new Truck view, we want to tell the database to begin using the Truck table.

All of our views assume they are initially started with a key, meaning that a Truck view is always opened on an existing truck, a Freight view is opened on an existing freight manifest, and so on. When we implemented the plug-in functions in Chapter 6 it caused us a small problem in that we had to provide a series of List views to allow the user to select an existing object or create a new object before we actually presented the main view. We found it was difficult to use the main view to fill in a new object when the view presupposed the object already existed.

Much of the logic we implemented in the previous chapter will serve us well here. The requirements in initializing and presenting the view are much the same, regardless of whether we get the data from a database or from a data bucket in the prototype. We need to clearly indicate the points at which we would expect to communicate with the database and to ensure that the communication with our psuedo-database operates in a manner compatible with the real database.

The easiest way to do this is to construct a new object, Pseudo-Database, which we will use to manage all of the data entered into and later displayed within views. All the views will need some modification to ensure they play by the new rules we will be imposing. These new rules will determine how and when data may be modified in these views and what will happen when the modifications are made. We are now attempting to prototype the real database interface logic. We can no longer allow the user to arbitrarily modify view data because uncontrolled modifications could corrupt the database. As an example, consider if the user were to change the destination of some freight after it has made it halfway to its final destination. Even if the change to the freight manifest were legitimate, changing the destination could corrupt information about the trucks and warehouses the freight was originally expected to pass through. We must therefore identify exactly what changes to data in the views are legal and what actions must be taken when each view is changed.

Analyzing the Freight View

As in previous chapters, I will concentrate primarily on the freight view, showing the steps you must follow to enhance the prototype. In this case it is important to remember we are dealing with two distinct situations: the first involving operations necessary to create a new waybill, and the second involving operations necessary to alter an existing waybill. The alteration of data is a trivial case because there is no valid reason to allow the user to alter any of the data shown in a waybill other than the destination. While there might be a few cases when a hysterical customer calls informing he or she has sent the wrong thing to the wrong place, we can find absolutely no reason for the interim destination list to be modified in the context of the waybill. This isn't to say the intermediate destinations cannot be altered, only that these destinations are a function of the trucks that transport the freight, therefore these modifications are more properly made in the views of the trucks themselves. In short, from the system's point of view, trucks determine where freight goes, freight does not determine where trucks go.

Although this is not a tome on formal analysis, I would like to stress one point often overlooked. All successful systems have a clearly defined logic, but this logic may not be quite the same as the logic of the real-world system they model or support. Considering our previous observations of the system's point of view about trucks and freight, many people would observe that without freight there is no reason for the trucks to go anywhere and so, it is the freight that determines where the trucks go. This is unarguably true, as Schroeder's livelihood is moving freight from one point to another based on customers' orders. However, this gives rise to another possibility, namely, that it is the customer who determines where freight, and therefore, trucks go.

The issue at the center of this conflict is the fact that the logic of the system can be defined in many ways, depending on one's point of view. It is the job of the skilled developer to identify the correct point of view in these cases and to ensure they conform with that point of view, no matter how ridiculous their statements may appear to some other viewpoint. The developer must also recognize all of these separate viewpoints and be capable of translating between them. Even though it may appear that the customer, Schroeder personnel, and the freight management system have three completely different ideas about what governs the behavior of freight and trucks, they are all discussing the same system and there must be a common denominator between them.

The crux of the issue is that there is a large difference between the behavior of a system, composed of Schroeder's customers, employees, and MIS systems, and the definitions of the system's behavior. The system functions as a single integrated entity, while each element of it attempts to describe the behavior of the entire system in terms of cause and effect. This means you should always select your viewpoint based on the "group" you are communicating with. When determining the system's behavior (as we are doing in this chapter) the system's viewpoint is the one you should adopt, whereas when you are talking to a Schroeder employee you should use their viewpoint and when talking to a customer you should use theirs. But if you try to tell your customers that the trucks determine where their freight goes, they will not trust you with their packages, as they might rightly feel you'll deliver them anywhere. And if you design the system with the idea that customers determine where trucks go, you are going to have a horribly inefficient freight routing system, not to mention a requirement for trucks exceeding Detroit's annual production.

We will now examine each of the components of the Waybill view, determining exactly what operations we will support in creating and editing waybills and how we expect these operations to interact with the existing database.

Addresses

The first thing that comes to mind in examining the addresses shown in the view is that the origin address is connected to a customer and shouldn't be edited at all, at least within the context of the Waybill view. Using common sense and then poking around in the database to confirm our assumptions, we find that the origin address isn't even stored in the Waybill table, it's stored in the Customer table. For this reason alone we want to prevent the user from altering the address in the Waybill view.

If they really want to do this, they should be doing it through the Customer view. When the user is entering information for a new waybill we don't want them to type in an address for the origin; we want them to indicate which customer is shipping the freight and we will then retrieve that customer's address from the database. The destination address will have to be entered directly by the user when a new waybill is being created or modified. The prime caveat here is that we should ensure the freight routing system is informed when the address is changed so it can recompute the intermediate destination list based on this new address.

In the interest of brevity, we will assume that this simple-minded solution is acceptable to our client, though in reality we know that such a solution rarely is. Changing the destination of a piece of freight in midstream is likely to be a complex action, one that could have far reaching effects on our design. Issues such as this one make rapid prototyping valuable because we might have to change a great deal of our assumptions. Consider a company policy where if a destination is changed while a piece of freight is in transit, then the original waybill is changed to make the next warehouse the final destination and a new waybill is created that routes the freight from this warehouse to the new final destination. If this were the case, we would have to modify our design to support such things as individual items of freight covered by multiple waybills and we would have to allow warehouses as final destinations. While we will not do that here, it might be instructive for you to work out how you would modify the existing design to support these requirements. Given the flexibility of the RP approach, in conjunction with the patience of high level OOL's such as Smalltalk, you shouldn't find this task too difficult.

Priority

The most obvious thing about the priority assigned to a piece of freight is that it is a known quantity to everybody. Unlike addresses, which tend to be unique to each customer, there are only a few clearly defined priorities in the system and they are applied equally to every freight item, regardless of who the customer is or where the freight is going. Our analysis of Schroeder's operations provided us with the list of priority codes and associated explanations, which are presented from least to highest priority in Table 7-1.

Table 7-1: Priority codes for Schroeder's operations.

Code	Description
Best Way	The cheapest, albeit slowest way
Standard	Default priority
Express	Attempt to be quick
Urgent	Attempt to be very quick
Rush	Damn the cost, get it there yesterday

Given these codes, we know we aren't going to let the user type anything they want into the priority field, instead we will present them with the five terms, allowing them to select one of the terms from the list. Additionally, since we know the majority of our shipments default to standard priority, we can assume this is the case for every new waybill and automatically fill out the field in this way. The user can ignore the priority field entirely unless they have a special reason to modify it. As we aren't going to be receptive to the modification of a freight item's priority in mid transit, we have to be somewhat clever here. Because we fill out the priority field with standard information when we create a new Waybill view, we need to know that we have done this and allow the user to change it before they actually file the waybill in the database; at that point they will no longer be able to change it. There is a fairly simple solution to this problem. We need to keep a Boolean flag around in the view supporting code, named something like NewManifest, and which is set True whenever the user is filling in a new freight manifest they haven't yet posted to the database and False at all other times. This is a tactical detail we are learning from our prototyping activities; it is concerned with the nitty gritty details of actually making the software work as opposed to being concerned with directly implementing our client's wishes.

Dates and Times

The next issues are the date and time fields that tell us when the freight was received and when the freight is due to be delivered. This is enough information to hang us. Consider if someone calls with a piece of freight going across town, but says it isn't to be delivered until next month. Does this mean that we should be smart enough to automatically warehouse it for a month?

Happily, the answer is no. The customer doesn't tell us the due date, we get that information from the freight scheduler after it has computed the intermediate destination list. This is a field we will calculate and we will then inform the customer when they can expect their freight shipment to be delivered. The time due field can be specified by the customer, but is simply a courtesy to them and allows us to know when they expect to be around to sign for their package. In terms of the overall operation of the system, it's meaningless data. We can allow the user to modify it at will because we don't care if they specify it in the first place.

The date received field is a little more complex—it is actually two dates in one. It is automatically filled out with the current date when the new waybill is created, determining the WaybillOrderDate. It will later be modified by the user, providing us another date, the Ship-Date. Because of the fact that we have two dates and only one field to show them in, we will simply set down the rule that after the waybill is initially created, we will always show the ShipDate. If the user wants to see the other dates, they can run a report on the database. This situation illustrates the fact that throughout the prototyping process you are going to be coming across new pieces of data and you will have to make decisions about what to do with them. When you are out in the field coding solutions to your client's problems, don't cast anything but the core structure of your design in concrete. As much as you cannot afford to alter your core assumptions, you also cannot be unwilling to modify the characteristics of individual pieces of the system. If this were the real world, we would most likely modify the freight manifest view so that it showed both the date the order was received and the date the freight was picked up.

Current Location and Intermediate Destinations

The current location display, along with the previous and future intermediate destination lists are both generated by the freight routing system and cannot be directly modified by the user. The information displayed in these fields is calculated initially when the waybill is first posted in the database and may be modified at will by the freight routing system in order to adapt to such things as truck delays and changes in final destination. For our purposes, we can ignore this information.

Design Evolution

What we just finished doing is limiting the scope of operations we will support. When we designed the prototype and demonstrated our dummy windows to the client, we were pretty loose about these requirements because we wanted to provide the user with as much flexibility as possible. We have now spent some time deliberately removing a part of this flexibility. Flexibility is not hard to provide in a RP environment, on the contrary, it is a natural component. Recall in Chapter 6 when we implemented the plug-in methods for the Waybill view, that we dealt with each of the display elements as an individual entity in its own right and attempted to provide each element with the same rough level of functionality. For example, we identified that the origin and destination addresses were both text fields, so we plugged in the built-in Smalltalk text editing facilities, giving the user the ability to change the data shown in either of these fields. Now we are further along and have decided that the origin address is generated by the user's selection of an existing customer from a list of known customers, thereby preventing the user from using the editing functions at all.

In many design and development environments this would be considered a criminal waste of resources because we spent a fair amount of time implementing editing functions for the origin address, only to discard them in the future. In the OOP environment, where one has ready access to a large library of classes that can already perform these various tasks for you, you don't spend much time writing code like this anyway. Instead, you spend time simply deciding what you will and will not use. Your time investment is much less than it would be in a more conventional environment. Additionally, given the reusable nature of code developed in the OOP environment, even if you were to decide not to use code you had previously written to satisfy an apparent requirement, you would not necessarily be dumping this code in the trash heap. If you had done a good job, it would be there in the future, patiently waiting for the time you needed it.

Whereas in most languages you start with a very limited system that slowly evolves to the desired degree of sophistication, the OOP environment already provides you with many sophisticated general purpose objects such as list managers and text editors. Instead of adding functionality to the system as you progress, many of your later decisions will deal with functionality *to be removed* from the system. In developing in the RP environment, you must always remember that in many cases it is much easier to restrict the operations of a general purpose solution to the problem; for example, it is easier to remove the editing controls from a text editor window than it is to add features to an initially special purpose solution. At first we observed that an address is a block of text so we could use the existing text editor class to support our address operations. Now we have observed, at least in the case of origin addresses, this text cannot be directly edited. We are moving slowly from a general description of an address to a more specific description, rather than starting of with a specific description and constantly adding more detail to it. Designing a program in this environment is much like sculpture—it isn't what you put on, it's what you take off.

Workflow

Up to now, we have been examining the fields of the Waybill view as distinct elements, not considering too much about how these fields relate to each other or to the system as a whole. We have considered the relationships of individual fields to the database, but only in terms of how each field is connected to its own private part of the database. Given that the database deals with records which describe entire waybills, we must now consider how the Waybill view as a whole relates to the database and to the rest of the system.

This involves *workflow*, or the orderly sequencing of operations across the view. If we decide to change the destination address, for example, this implies that certain other things must happen. We must inform the database we are changing the address so it will be updated correctly and we must inform the freight routing system about the change so it can redo the intermediate destination list.

In dealing with workflow, one of the most important things to know is when to stop. For example, in changing the final destination for a piece of freight in this view, we are also changing the loading manifests for every truck currently in the future intermediate destination list. For us to discuss this here would bring in far too many details. A good rule of thumb when dealing with OOP systems is that you simply need to deal with the effects on the object you are considering and any objects this particular object is directly linked to. Although we know that the truck manifests will have to be changed, we can ignore that because we aren't directly linked to them. We are directly linked to the freight routing system and we are obliged to inform it that we have changed the final destination. We can assume that the freight routing system, or something it is connected to, will ensure that the manifests are correctly updated. Therefore, we can concern ourselves with those elements with which we must directly interact.

We will divide the analysis of the workflow into two distinct parts: the workflow in creating a new freight manifest and the workflow in editing an existing freight manifest. We will do this because in the first case the workflow is fairly clearly defined and in the second there might not even be any workflow (if the user is simply examining an existing manifest).

Creating a Freight Manifest

In creating a freight manifest, we can assume three things about our starting condition: the system has presented an empty Freight Manifest view, it knows we are creating a new manifest (see the NewManifest flag described above), and a new waybill number has been generated and assigned automatically.

The first step is to fill in the known default information. This involves placing the value Standard in the priority field and today's date in the date received field. If we want to be especially helpful, we could put the word Unscheduled into the current destination display to help users understand that freight that has no destination or origin is tough to schedule.

Following this, we need to set the origin address. As stated, we don't want the user directly entering the origin address in the field, instead we want them to select a customer and we will then fetch the customer's address from the database and place it in this field. For this reason, we will need to automatically display a list of customers to the user—the list is centered on top of the Freight Manifest view. If they select a customer, we will then obtain their address and place it in the origin address. If they fail to select a customer we will terminate the construction of the new freight manifest. In cases where a new customer must be created before they can be selected, we will employ the same solution we used to solve the problem of creating new freight manifests. The first line in the customer list will say something like

```
New Customer...
```

and if the user selects that line they will be presented with a customer view to be filled out before they return to the current freight manifest view.

Now that they have created a new customer, we want to get them to enter the destination of the freight. We will force them into the destination address display area and we will keep them there until they type something. Following this, we will allow them the opportunity to move about the display and modify the priority and the date received, should they so desire.

Following the user's entry of the destination address, there is no more information they are required to give us, so we must provide them with a way to indicate that they are finished entering data. My preferred mechanism in such cases is to have a button within the view that says "OK" or "Done."

What takes place after this button is pressed is also part of the workflow. We must inform the database that we have a new freight manifest record which needs to be created and we must also inform the freight routing system so it can calculate the intermediate destinations and give us an idea of when the freight will be delivered. The best way to do this, given that we know the database is central to all system operations, is to file the new freight manifest in the database and then to have the freight routing system compute the intermediate destination list and delivery time from the newly created record. It will then add its own data to this record and return control to the code controlling the Freight Manifest view. When we regain control, we remove the "OK" button, load the new data from the database, and update the intermediate destination lists and date due fields accordingly. At this point we have left the creation workflow sequence and have entered the editing or viewing workflow sequence.

Editing a Freight Manifest

As editing is by no means as structured an activity as filling out the freight manifest, the definition of the workflow is correspondingly fuzzy. When this is combined with the fact that the most of the fields are not editable anyway, this leaves us with a rather short list of possible workflows.

Notice that I have said a *short list of workflows,* as in more than one workflow. In the case of editing elements of the freight manifest, we really must define a workflow for each element the user might modify. We cannot merge all of these together into a master workflow for the simple reason that we do not know which, if any, of the fields the user will modify. We must therefore define an individual workflow for every field the user can modify, which numbers one in this case.

We stated earlier that we would allow the operator to change the destination of a piece of freight, assuming that we had not already delivered it. The workflow for this is fairly simple, as soon as we have detected that the user has modified the destination address, we inform the database of the change, and then recalculate the manifest route from the current location to the new destination.

Summary

Up to this point, we have had a great deal of flexibility in determining the behavior of the system. This isn't to say we can dictate the behavior of the system as we are attempting to implement the client's wishes; more that we haven't had anything forcing requirements down our throats. In this chapter we see that this is not always true, especially in cases where a new piece of software must operate with an existing system.

You don't want to begin dealing with this issue until you are starting to get the basic behavior of your system worked out because you don't want this external system dictating the overall behavior of your system. While you have to ensure that your system plays by the rules imposed by the external system, you don't want to have your system's entire operating characteristics determined by this system.

One nice thing in dealing with external systems is that you usually aren't dealing with the kind of fuzzy issues we've been handling up to now. Instead, the external system has very specific requirements and they are often quite clearly defined. In situations like these you want to leave the fuzzy RP style of design and return to the traditional analysis tools. In doing this, you should be operating under the assumption that you are designing a *gateway* between your new system and the existing system it must interact with.

In dealing with an external system imposing rigid requirements on you, you'll find that you will have to alter the behavior of your software to meet these requirements. This is where you will come to truly appreciate the class hierarchy found in many OO systems because you aren't forced to throw out general capabilities you have spent a lot of time implementing. Instead, you will simply have to suppress some capabilities you inherited from the supplied class hierarchy. In this chapter, we saw how certain text editing functions have to be locked down. This isn't too painful because you didn't have to write text editing functions to begin with.

Workflow is an important issue when dealing with external systems, especially when those systems reflect more of a procedural mindset than the standard OO program. Most OO programs are hard to flowchart because the individual objects respond to messages triggered by user actions in the interface, and there really isn't any specific path we force the user to go through in the interface. Therefore, the overall sequential behavior of the program is largely a function of what the user decides to do and when they decide to do it.

This doesn't work so well with systems that expect the user to perform things in some rigid order. When this is the case, you will have to clearly define what the order is that the user is expected to accomplish a task in, and then make sure that logic is added to OO system so that this order is followed. There is no simple solution to this problem; you will have to analyze the workflow requirements and add logic to the system to enforce them each time you encounter such a situation. In short, this particular situation reflects the meeting of a modeless object-oriented system with a system that proceeds from one specific state to another.

- Try to have your system have its own *identity* before you start dealing with external systems.
- External systems can often make rigid demands on the behavior of your system, demands that may appear to be arbitrary and capricious.
- Traditional analysis tools work better than RP techniques in dealing with such situations.
- The first step in dealing with an external system is to *lock down* everything you can, based on the demands of the external system. What you can lock down can be ignored from then on.
- What cannot be locked down must be sequenced based on the requirements of the external system.
- This is much like sculpture. You don't want to deal with situations like this by adding capabilities unless you have to. You want to remove capabilities to satisfy the external requirements.

Exercises

1. Take one of your windows and configure it so that the user must follow a specific editing sequence. In short, make them modify one field, then another, and so on. Do not allow them to pick any field for modification, instead allow them access to only the next or the previous field.

2. If you feel bold, try to integrate your windows with an external DBMS. If you don't have a DBMS, build a simple record manager using the String and IndexedCollection classes to emulate a DBMS, and then integrate this with your windows.

CHAPTER 8

Standing on the Shoulders of Others

How do you eat an elephant?
One bite at a time.

As I noted in the introduction to this book, my primary intent is not to teach you the tactical mechanics of programming in an OOL, rather it is to illustrate the strategy of rapid prototyping. For this reason, this book's text to code ratio is much higher than books that are focused more on the tactical details of implementing a program in the language they are discussing. You may have noticed that as this book has progressed I have provided less code, focusing on "softer" issues involved in the design and implementation of the prototype. My intent is that you use this book in conjunction with a good tutorial on Smalltalk so you will have a complete strategic/tactical package to work from.

All this aside, in this chapter I will focus on some of the details of the Smalltalk environment. I should stress that my intent is not to teach you the tactics of programming in Smalltalk; instead, I want to illustrate the higher level issues involved in object-oriented programming in general. At this point you may feel that I have left you without guidance to implement all of these wonderful things. To some extent this is true. I am not going to show you the exact code that solves the tasks that have been laid out so far, as I feel that in prototyping, the exact code produced by each programmer is a matter of personal style. All underlying algorithms are the same, but there are many legitimate ways to produce code realizations of them.

In any case, if you feel you don't really know where to start, fear not. You are already better off than those that have gone charging ahead, blindly producing code before looking around and cataloging their resources.

The Class Hierarchy

I assume that this book isn't your first encounter with the concepts of object-oriented programming. You should be comfortable with the idea of class hierarchy, especially as it applies to inheritance between related classes. I will concentrate on two areas not always discussed in introductions to the class hierarchy, specifically the act of *browsing the hierarchy*, and the construction of *reusable generic code*.

Grazing in the Class Hierarchy

Although much has been said about the use of OOL's to create and share common class libraries, there are many object-oriented packages that do not come with any kind of class hierarchy. To my mind, this defeats the whole purpose of the object-oriented paradigm, which is the sharing of general purpose code that solves problems encountered in most, if not all, software development projects. If you were to switch from developing software in C to developing software in C++, without acquiring a common class library at the same time, you would be missing the best part of the system.

When developing in an object-oriented environment and especially when doing rapid prototyping, you should expect to spend the majority of your time in the library doing research. The production of code in this environment is much different from the production of code in traditional environments. Your focus changes from knowing how to implement solutions to requirements to knowing where to look for implementations that already exist in the library.

As an example, consider if you were writing a training program to help teach young children basic math skills. In order to provide the teacher with information about the performance of each child, your experience tells you that you need to create some kind of keyed list which keeps the necessary information for each child. In the traditional environment, you will usually find some easy way to accomplish this, such as having the teacher define all of the students by name and number and then have students select themselves from the list as they start using the software. Your basic objective is to keep the solution simple because your primary job is to produce a training program, not a database manager for student test scores.

In an object-oriented environment with an extensive class hierarchy, your objectives remain the same, but your options are vastly expanded. Generalizing the definition of the test database, what we really want to do is to create a *collection* of student scores, where each element of the collection provides scoring information on the student. The optimal solution would be something like a dictionary, where each student's name is a key in the dictionary and the scoring information is stored under these keys.

As it so happens, most class libraries worthy of the name contain a large subtree with a very general purpose collection class at the root. In Smalltalk there is a Collection class which is derived directly from the Object class. Under the Collection class you will find a horde of special-purpose collection engines, from simple-minded creatures like Bags, Sets, and Strings, to more complex entities such as Dictionaries, OrderedCollections, and LinkedLists. In fact, the Collection subtree is often the largest part of a class hierarchy, as so many software tasks primarily involve the management of collections of data.

The main issue here is that you can quickly solve the score database requirement by using one of the existing classes in the library, as opposed to working harder and taking longer implementing your own private solution to the problem. In order to do this, you must know what resources are available to you in the class hierarchy.

I cannot overstress this issue. It was first brought to light by Dr. Adele Goldberg, one of the original designers of the Smalltalk language in a very non-traditional (because it was readable) paper titled *The Programmer as a Reader*. Her point was simple, although it still seems to have been lost on the industry as a whole. When we teach students to write, we do this only after having taught them to read. If I were to propose that the student who had never read any literature stood the same chance of writing the next great novel as a student with a good foundation in existing literature, you would correctly inform me that I was an idiot. However, in the computer business we expect to create great programmers who have never read anything other than fragments of a whole program not of their own creation.

On one hand you can't blame us. Forcing someone to read 500,00 lines of a COBOL accounting program is an impossible and tortuous task. But it also means that programmers cannot learn the techniques of others by reading their work; instead, they must rediscover these techniques themselves. In many environments it is the only solution, but it is an expensive solution.

In the OOP environment things are different. Programs are composed of cooperating objects so there is little point in reading such a program in entirety, at least with a highly detailed focus. In order to learn from it, you concentrate first on the capabilities of the individual objects and then you move to understanding how objects interact with each other to form the program as a whole. What is important is that the behavior of the objects stays consistent across the applications that use them. In other words, although you may use a Dictionary object one day to implement your test score catalog for a piece of training software and may use a Dictionary object another day to carry freight manifests, the behavior of the Dictionary object stays consistent across the applications. This is due to the fact that the definition of the Dictionary object is in terms of a specific kind of collection, as opposed to a special piece of code in a specific application.

Programmers already do this to a limited extent, as we all use common function libraries such as the standard C library in C programming environments. Nobody bothers writing a square root function, we know it's in the library and we use it when we need it. But in C, as in most languages, the construction of general purpose libraries is somewhat of an art form and the majority of each application is custom code written to solve the specific problems of the application. Object-oriented programs, on the other hand, are composed primarily of general purpose code from the existing class hierarchy, with a smaller amount of specialized code that deals with the issues particular to the specific application.

When working in an object-oriented environment, you must change your problem solving approach. Instead of confronting a requirement and immediately determining what algorithm you will have to implement to satisfy the requirement, you should attempt to redefine the requirement in as generalized terms as you possibly can. Following this, you want to read through the parts of the class hierarchy to determine which parts may already implement solutions for all or part of your problem.

In order to do this successfully, you must be comfortable with reading code written by others. You should understand how the class hierarchy is arranged and what its strengths and weaknesses are. The only way you can do this is if you have read through the hierarchy.

Techniques of Browsing

There are certain specific techniques in browsing that will help you reach this efficiency. By following these basic steps, you will gain the greatest familiarity with the hierarchy with the least amount of effort. In order to understand the hierarchy, it is not necessary for you to read every bit of code in it right now; instead, you need to form a "mental model" of the hierarchy so that as you read bits and pieces of it over time, you can integrate the new information together with what you have previously learned so you are always in possession of a single cohesive understanding of the hierarchy.

The first step is to completely ignore the innards of all the classes and concentrate on how the classes are grouped together in the hierarchy. As you do this, you will be able to discern large subgroups in the hierarchy that deal with related concepts. After all, that's the whole point of inheritance.

In the case of Smalltalk, you will find that some of the more obvious groupings cover the management of collections of data, the manipulation of quantities, the display of information, and the control of the user interface. Table 8-1 summarizes these subtrees as they are found in the Smalltalk/V environment, though it is by no means complete.

Table 8-1: Some Smalltalk/V subtrees.

Class Name	Purpose
Collection	Collections of data from the simple to the sublime
Magnitude	Numbers, measurements, time, date, and space
Pane	The display of information on the screen
Dispatcher	User interface control, keyboard, and mouse inputs

You should now begin to scan through these subtrees to understand how the designers have moved from the general to the more specific as they continued to subclass elements of the tree. For example, you will find that the Magnitude class deals with things that are common to all quantities, regardless of whether they represent Dates, Times, or Numbers. Further down this hierarchy you will find the Number class, which deals with concepts common to all numbers, but not necessarily common to all Magnitudes. And still further down you will find the Float class, which deals with the peculiarities of floating-point numbers. As you do this, you have yet to read any actual Smalltalk code, except for the class and method names themselves. But your explorations are showing you what kinds of capabilities each of the classes have and how these capabilities are related to each other through the class hierarchy.

As you do this, it often helps to implement some "toy" programs so that you have "real" reasons for wandering through the hierarchy. This is due to the fact that one learns more from directed exploration, rather than through random exploration. There is a drawback, however, in that you will end up understanding the behavior of some parts of the hierarchy much better than you will the behavior of others. If you have first scanned the overall hierarchy so you can form a mental image of where the pieces fit, this really isn't much of a nuisance, as you will know how to file away all of the information you learn in the future. It is much easier to form and fine tune this model by trying to accomplish small tasks than it is to wander aimlessly through the hierarchy. Once you have the model, you can effectively deal with learning the hierarchy on a "need to know" basis. I've been programming in Smalltalk for many years and I still don't know anything about certain sections of the hierarchy because I've never had any reason to use them.

At this point, you are becoming a "reader" of code. Instead of trying to personally implement solutions to every problem you confront, you are now going through the class hierarchy, reading about what others have done and determining if that will help you solve your problem. In many cases you will find help within the hierarchy, for no other reason than the bulk of the code in the hierarchy makes it statistically likely. You can now proceed to the final step of educated browsing: experimentation.

I make it a policy, at least once a week, to wander through sections of the class hierarchy I am using and examine the more bizarre methods that may be found within it. In Smalltalk, the richest ground for exploration are the Pane and Dispatcher classes, especially the methods that support communications between panes and their associated dispatchers. You will find methods in here that implement all sorts of strange behaviors, ones that you may feel you'll never use. But you should experiment with the ones that tickle your fancy, simply to see exactly what they do and how they do it. This educated experimentation will keep you from becoming stuck in a rut by showing you new ideas and new ways to do things. These ways may not necessarily be good in your eyes, but that really isn't important. They are definitely *different* from the ways in which you do things because they were written by somebody else. For this reason alone, they have the potential to help push you over hurdles you may encounter.

Writing Reusable Code

Only after you have learned to read other peoples code and become familiar with what is available to you in the class hierarchy, can you begin to create *reusable* code. Reusable code is one of the most powerful concepts in the object-oriented language paradigm, for it means that once you have solved a particular problem you never need to solve the same problem again. You just reuse your original solution.

As you learn the existing class hierarchy, you are also learning about the construction of reusable code; the entire class hierarchy is nothing but reusable code. None of it is specific to one application, save for that fraction which is used to directly implement the Smalltalk language and custom environmental features. The creation of reusable code requires a deeper understanding of the nature of the code so that you can separate the general from the specific. Usually, you're trying to solve some application-specific problem and are attempting to get as much general purpose code as you can from the solution of the application requirements.

This is indeed the crux of the issue, the fact that reusable or generic code is being produced in the process of developing a specific application. It requires you to use both insight and foresight to ensure you clearly separate what is unique to the application from what is of general use to the programming community at large. To complicate this issue, there is no clear dividing line where code on one side is reusable and code on the other side is not. Instead, you have code that is reusable, code that isn't reusable, and code that is somewhat reusable.

For example, one area of the freight management system we have not directly addressed, is the freight routing system. In order to solve a routing problem, you will need to research graph analysis algorithms and, if you are like me, you may settle on Prim's algorithm to actually perform the routing calculation, figuring the least cost path from the origin to the destination. In doing this you will probably refer to dusty tomes like the Association for Computing Machineries (ACM) Collected Algorithms library and you will probably end up creating a Graph subclass of the Collection class, with the subclass knowing how to perform these desired operations. Now, is this code reusable or isn't it? The answer is, "It depends." If you have been a good programmer and studiously avoided embedding freight-specific details in the Graph class, then yes, the Graph class is reusable code, at least in applications that care about graph analysis.

This situation clearly illustrates the two central issues in the construction of reusable code, the first being the careful avoidance of inserting application-specific details where they don't belong and the second being the overall usefulness of the new capabilities to future applications.

Separation of Application Details

In creating reusable code, the most important thing to do is to separate all code into two sections: one containing details of interest only to the current application and the second containing details of interest to any application attempting to perform a similar task. Returning to the freight routing system, we know that we will have to implement some type of graph analysis algorithm to solve the routing problem. We can instantly reject creating a method within the Freight or Truck classes to accomplish this, as that would obviously bind our solution to the application and force us to reimplement it whenever we needed a similar capability in the future.

Unfortunately, this is where many novice object-oriented pro-grammers stop, assuming that they are now creating wonderful reus-able code. They will then implement a Graph class or something similar, which knows how to perform routing between the various warehouses by extracting the origin and destination addresses from the manifest. In short, they will implement a method such as

```
route: aFreightManifest
```

where the method extracts the origin and destination addresses from the freight manifest parameter and then uses the internal database to generate the routing information. They might as well have just stuffed the whole thing into one of the application classes, as it is still quite application specific, of use only in determining routes for the Schroe-der Trucking company. If an express mail company called with an in-terest in the product, about the only thing we would have gained from this exercise is the metrics on how long it takes to write the method from scratch. Given the previous solution to the routing prob-lem, that's exactly what we will be doing: writing the same piece of code again from scratch. A more experienced object-oriented software house will not have made this mistake, will have underbid us on the new contract, and we will be watching our company lose to the com-petition.

It is not sufficient to say that since this is a general purpose utility we will create it as a subclass of an existing generic class. That state-ment is false for two reasons. First, as all classes are in the end derived from the Object class, then all application classes are derived from ge-neric reusable classes. Second, many application-specific classes are defined as subclasses of generic system classes because they modify the behavior of the generic class in some application-specific way. Considering our earlier example of the student scores dictionary, we could envision the creation of a new dictionary subclass that re-sponded to requests for raw scores, scores graded on a curve, and so on. The claim that a class is reusable because it is derived from a reusable class is meaningless. All classes are derived from reusable classes and this fact has nothing to do with the reusability of classes with one specific exception. It is generally true that a class derived from an application-specific class is not reusable. The average programmer, however, is more than capable of recognizing this condition and is rarely trapped by it.

Reusability arises from the conscious choice to make a class reusable and the focused effort to ensure that the class contains no application-specific details. If we want to make a truly reusable graph class, we must ensure that it does not depend on the presence of our application in any way. This means we should not expect it to understand our application's private objects, such as the FreightManifest, and we should not expect it to implicitly share data with our application, such as the database of adjacent warehouses. The message to a reusable Graph class to perform routing might be:

```
routeFrom: <origin> to: <destination> in: <network>
```

where the network parameter provides a set of two element records that define all of the adjacent nodes in a network, and origin and destination specify the two nodes the route should be generated between. Considering a toy route on the west coast, the actual call might be:

```
routeFrom: 'San Diego' to: 'Seattle'
    in: #(('San Diego' 'Los Angeles')
                ('Los Angeles' 'San Francisco')
                ('San Francisco' 'Portland')
                ('Portland' 'Seattle'))
```

Reading and Reusability: The Divide and Conquer Approach

Now that you have seen the benefits of reading code written by others and reusing all the code you possibly can, the last remaining detail involves what happens when these two approaches are combined. When discussing reusability you usually find yourself in a quest for the production of reusable code while writing an application that was not intended to be reusable. In short, how does one overcome the fact that the quest for generic behavior takes place in an environment whose goal is to have very specific behavior?

As you design and implement your system, regardless of whether you do it in a prototyping environment or in a final production environment, you must always attempt to decompose your problems into their elemental components. Much of this will come naturally to you as an object-oriented programmer, for this is the way in which you create any new class. But there are certain steps you should take in order to gain the greatest possible effects, vis-à-vis not duplicating someone else's work and not forcing someone else to duplicate yours.

As you examine the various requirements you are trying to satisfy, do not assume that they are indivisible units. Instead, you should always try to divide the requirements into two sections, the first being the stuff common to most applications and the second being the stuff unique to the current application. You should then continue to repeat this process with whatever you have determined is application specific until you simply cannot divide the problem any more.

When you have completed this, carefully examine the reasons behind your decisions to call something an application-specific requirement. What you are seeking is a determination of whether the operation as a whole is unique to the application or if the application simply performs some standard operation in a novel way. The reason for this step is simple, it will determine whether you must start a large new class implementing all of the necessary logic to implement your application-specific task, or whether you need to subclass an existing class in order to change its behavior.

Consider if we were dealing with the integration of accounting utilities into our freight management system. Many accounting systems use internal accounting numbers, where the numbers are divided in such a way to allow one to quickly determine what kind of account is being used. For example, numbers between 1,000 and 2,000 might be customer billing accounts, 2,000 and 3,000 capital expenditures, and so on. If we wanted to construct a hierarchical database where the top level broke the accounts down by the thousands and then the next levels broke out the individual accounts, we would be tempted to construct a class from scratch to satisfy this requirement. After all, the requirement, as stated, doesn't seem to match up to any of our existing generic classes.

Actually, there is another option, one that involves far less work because it reuses many of the capabilities already present in the class hierarchy. We can create a new subclass of Dictionary, called AccountingDictionary, and override the normal behavior of dictionaries in order to achieve the following goals:

- Account numbers are used as keys in the dictionary
- An account number is rounded down to the nearest thousand and then this value is used to retrieve a new dictionary, stored within the current dictionary
- The rounded account number is subtracted from the original account number (effectively a remainder 1,000 operation) and this value is used to retrieve the actual account information from the dictionary we retrieved in the previous step

Instead of creating a whole new class from scratch, we got the same result by overriding the normal keying behavior of the Dictionary class.

Summary

My intent in previous chapters has not been to provide you with reams of code that you can dutifully type into your computer in order to achieve the desired effect. I assume that if you are studying such things as object-oriented programming and rapid prototyping, you are already sick and tired of doing things this way and are looking for a better approach. Instead, what I have done is to present you with problems that are similar to capabilities that already exist in the class library, although I have added some twists and turns to these problems. If you take the approaches I have illustrated here and apply them to the things we have discussed and will be discussing, you will find that there is nowhere near as much work involved as you might have thought. If you try to do everything yourself, you have a monumental task in front of you. If, on the other hand, you realize that this project is no more complex than the Smalltalk environment itself and is quite similar to it in many ways, you can effectively use the class hierarchy to do your job for you.

Traditional programming is a process of raw construction, where you start with very little and hack away until you have completely defined the brand new world that is the application. This entire process is becoming more and more suspect these days as software becomes more and more complex. We are finding that definition to this degree has many of the same inherent flaws as does reduction to this degree. In short, the approach of *definitio ad absurdum*, brought to its peak by computer science, has many of the same flaws as *reductio ad absurdum*. We are simply discovering in software today what the subatomic physicists discovered in the early 20th century.

CHAPTER 9

A Meeting of Minds

Watch out for formal briefings, they often produce an avalanche.
(Definition: A high-level snow job of massive and overwhelming proportions.)

At this time, the prototype freight management system is operational, but sketchy. Given the information I have presented in previous chapters, in conjunction with the exercises at the end of chapters, you have a system that can pass itself off to the casual observer as the company's great new information management tool. Once again, it's time to take the prototype back to the client and let them try it out.

Rather than discuss what might occur in such a meeting, I shall focus on the role of the meetings themselves, discussing how they affect the software development process and the players involved, and how to interpret the spoken and unspoken goals of the meetings. The focus of this chapter is admittedly on "soft" or somewhat undefinable issues, but *this subject is critical in all software development* and particularly so in rapid prototyping environments. Remember, you are not writing this software for the computer that will be running it so much as you are for the people that will be using it. For this reason, you should pay attention to their wants and needs.

Goals: Strategic and Tactical

Although this is only the second client demonstration session I have directly alluded to in this book, it really isn't. It is the second *major* walkthrough. Between the first session and this follow-up, there should have been dozens of meetings with various client personnel at a lower and less formal level. In prototyping, there are two distinct kinds of client meetings; the first dealing with the extraction of information and ideas from clients and the second verifying that the first set of meetings was a success. I have stressed that modern software development often has little resemblance to the formal development process taught in schools and industry accepted texts. Instead, it's much more of a hit-or-miss affair, with everyone stumbling around in the dark, hoping that they will trip over the correct solution to the problems confronting them. This arises primarily from the fact that software development is innately a human process, as opposed to the mechanistic process many claim it to be. If such an argument were true there wouldn't be much need for programmers, as our current technology is well suited for automating mechanical tasks. When the task requires creativity and insight, our technology is of little use.

Because this is a creative process, we should recognize the need for constant interaction with the end users of the system. You should not expect to be handed a several hundred page document that clearly describes the client's desires; *you* will have to dig out these desires, detail by detail. In many cases the clients don't know exactly what they want, so part of your job is to help them learn what it is they want. In any successful prototyping environment you will have many meetings with the clients in order to extract information and ideas from them. These meetings are the driving force behind your prototyping efforts. You will find most of these meetings will be triggered by your inability to proceed with development until you get more information from the client. Consider the beginnings of this hypothetical project; there is little chance that you would have attempted to design the basic views we created without having a series of meetings with the client. If you didn't have the meetings, you wouldn't have the slightest idea of what windows to implement and what information to present in these windows. Fear not, the first kind of meetings always take care of themselves.

The second kind of meetings you will hold are of the type I have discussed already in the book and they always follow a fixed pattern. In the jargon of contract programming, they are often referred to as *headspace* or *sanity* checks and they are used to ensure you have correctly understood and used the information extracted from the clients. There are specific times you should hold these meetings and there is a distinct evolutionary pattern to them.

In order to distinguish between these two kinds of meetings, we will attach labels to each of them, making that quaint assumption that if you name something, you then must understand it. This first kind of meetings are *informational* meetings where the objective is the free exchange of information, but an exchange of information that does not directly involve decision making. The second kind of meetings are *walkthroughs*, where the goal is to define shared concepts and the current status of the project and where the end result is a series of decisions that bring all involved parties back into agreement.

Strategic Goals

I previously discussed a hypothetical meeting with Mr. Schroeder where we discussed our basic concept for the project, describing it as a sophisticated graphical system for the efficient tracking and management of the freight his company transports. In this meeting we presented the basic windows we expected the system to provide to the operator, using dummy data to show Mr. Schroeder how the operators could navigate through the information available to them. Our main focus however, was not to elicit approval for these windows, but for the concept they represented. Mr. Schroeder could care less about the sophistication of our software; in fact, as far as the software and computers are concerned, he views them only as tools that support his business of moving freight from point A to point B. His only interest in the software is whether or not it improves this movement.

Such meetings with senior members of the company should take place as soon as you have identified your objective and have assembled a small system or set of viewgraphs that clearly describes, in the client's terms, what this objective is. I recommend you build simple mockup prototypes, a prototype of a prototype if you will, for the simple reason that clients will find it easier to understand than computer jargon which could accidentally creep into a text description of your objective. The goal of such meetings is to have the client approve your objective, which means that you have successfully identified your strategic goal. Until you and the client agree on the overall strategic goal, there is little reason to develop detailed software—it won't be what they want. Rapidly prototyping a system that does not satisfy the client's strategic goals is simply a rapid path to failure.

The crux of this issue here, which defines the basic characteristics of these client meetings, is the distinction between *strategy* and *tactics*. In order to develop and field software successfully in the rapid prototyping environment, you must understand the difference between these two terms and understand how they are related to the evolution of your prototype. Rapid prototyping depends in large part on your flexibility, your ability to work in a difficult environment, and most of all, your ability to hunt down and extract the information you need in order to take the software from a rough idea to a concrete manifestation. To do this you must clearly identify your strategic and tactical goals, quickly and accurately.

The following is the best definition of strategy and tactics I've heard over the course of my career. While I'm sure the definition wasn't born with the man who told it to me, I am forever indebted to him for teaching it to me; it has been the one thing I have used every day of my career:

Strategy is deciding what you want to do, tactics deals with how this will be accomplished.

Let's reexamine our first meeting with Mr. Schroeder in light of this statement. We are seeking strategic approval from Mr. Schroeder, an agreement that we are working towards the same goal. An often-heard complaint of programmers is that the companies for which they design software have no understanding of their problems and that their goals and the companies' goals are different. This cannot be true if a project is to succeed. If you dig deep enough, your basic strategic goal is exactly the same as Mr. Schroeder's, to make money at what you do. If you don't help Mr. Schroeder meet his, you are unlikely to meet yours.

It was this logic that drove us to our initial meeting with Mr. Schroeder. There was little point on deciding any tactical issues until we verified that our strategic goal was appropriate. We extracted information from the company about what they did, what problems they were having, and what might alleviate these problems. With this information, we decided they needed some kind of integrated freight tracking system and we returned to Mr. Schroeder with this proposal and just enough software to illustrate the directions we wanted to take. After receiving his approval, we were free to begin concentrating on tactical goals.

Tactical Goals

The issue of tactical goals is subservient to the strategic goals, but they are also more complex because several sets of goals must be juxtaposed and they are goals that sometimes are contradictory. In dealing with tactical goals, we must deal with both our own tactical goals, which deal with the way we will implement the software and what effect this will have on the software's function, and the client's tactical goals, which deal with the ways in which they wish to interact with this software.

This is the second and final stage in the evolution of the walkthrough meetings. Whereas the initial strategic decisions are primarily controlled by the client, with inputs from the software developer limited to what is and is not technically possible, the tactical meetings are more balanced, with the developer and the client reaching a compromise.

While the primary client personnel involved in approving our strategic goals were high-level managers within the client organization, the personnel involved in the tactical meetings are those who are directly involved in the use of the new system or the operation of the freight transportation system itself. Their job is to ensure the system provides them with the information they need to do their jobs and does it in such a way that they can do their jobs more efficiently. The software developer's personnel at these meetings are there to ensure all of their wishes are met, but they also have a hidden agenda in that they represent the software, and make sure that no decisions are made at these meetings that detrimentally affect the software itself. For this reason, these meetings can sometimes disintegrate into shouting matches, as both sides come to battle over a point that cannot be satisfied without compromise from everyone.

The most critical issue is to determine how often these meetings should be held and what people should be involved. The best way to decide who should be involved is to evaluate those people you have used as information resources within the client organization and include them in most, if not all of these meetings. As to the frequency of the meetings, you probably want to use the cream of the crop on a fairly regular basis to help you catch any glaring errors before they become public spectacles.

We are left with one key type of meeting, which is the larger group review of the prototype's current capabilities and the developer's future plans for its evolution. Unlike the informational meetings and the smaller walkthrough meetings, these meetings are far more complex, primarily due to the far ranging effects of any decisions reached here. Informational meetings do not normally result in decisions and smaller walkthroughs involve less crucial decisions about things like the placement of fields in views. These larger meetings are used to decide larger issues, such as whether entire views or operational sequences should be inserted or dropped.

Major Walkthroughs

I have expressly chosen not to call this session a design review. This is not to cast aspersions at a design review, but to ensure that the focus here isn't on quibbling about whether some algorithm should have been implemented recursively or whether or not some particular loop is as efficient as it could be. While design reviews are valuable components in any software design effort, they address only the considerations of the program designers. End users don't care about loops and recursion, they care about whether or not they like the software.

An old client of mine once observed there were only three measurements that applied to software efficiency, and none of these had anything to do with the use of loops or recursion. He said that 1 second or less response time is OK, 2 second response times are a pain, and 3 seconds or more is simply too damn long!

This is the kind of observation you want and will get in walkthroughs with the staff because, unlike programmers, they are unconcerned with and oblivious to how the software works. They are concerned with the visible effects of decisions the developers have made. This attitude is a necessary counterbalance to more traditional design reviews, as it prevents decisions from being made that, while locally valid, are globally invalid. This keeps software developers focussed on the end product, as opposed to becoming wrapped up in the techniques that produce the end product.

Before proceeding, it is necessary to return to the object-oriented paradigm so that its direct relationship to this situation can be detailed. What I have said about the meetings with the staff applies equally to a COBOL development team as it does to a Smalltalk development team. What is different are the options available to the teams.

The COBOL team will attend the meeting, do their best to identify areas in the software that should be changed, and work to balance the conflicting demands presented by the staff. They leave with copious notes and then attempt to integrate all the demands and observations into a single integrated modification plan so that they can satisfy the largest number of people possible. Given the iterative nature of development in compiled languages such as COBOL, PL/1, and ADA, this is all that anyone can reasonably expect from them. Unfortunately, problems often arise because they misinterpret what the clients have been trying to say and when they return to the next meeting, the clients make the same demands again, often coupling these with new demands. Demands of the clients are expressed in a language such as English, which is open to many possible interpretations. The result of these demands is more COBOL code, which is open only to a single interpretation, the computers. Identifying which interpretation of the human language should be used is often a process of trial and error.

The rapid prototyping team however, has another option open to them if they are using a language such as Smalltalk. Given that the software is being physically demonstrated to the client, as opposed to being presented as a series of overheads, they can modify the system on the fly, literally adapting the system to the participant's demands as the demands are made. This isn't to say that everything is so easy in Smalltalk that any request can be instantly granted, just that demands that deal primarily with cosmetic or organizational issues can often be satisfied on the spot. In cases where the clients present multiple conflicting demands, each demand can be shown in turn. This allows the clients to see they are making conflicting demands and then to resolve amongst themselves which demand is to be satisfied.

There is one structural change to the general meeting that should be made. Traditionally, one goes to the client site, demonstrates and discusses the software with the client, takes a lot of notes, and then leaves to work on the changes. We have augmented this process somewhat by allowing for on-site modification of the software where the client demands can be rapidly satisfied. By changing the organization of the meeting, we can satisfy even more demands.

Large meetings usually take an entire day and are usually exhausting. If, however, the meeting is scheduled so that there is a session in the morning and a session in the afternoon, separated by a long lunch, the majority of the development team can work through lunch to modify the system to accommodate some of the client requests that were too complex to be instantly gratified, but not so complex as to require several days or more intensive effort. The central issue here is that you want to attack as many of these points as possible while they are fresh in everybody's minds, before time has passed and the issues have been muddied. Let the marketing people and a few of the technical staff go to lunch with the clients, but have a large component of the team stay behind to modify those parts of the system that can be changed in an hour or so.

The end result of this type of interaction with the staff is that the issues are dealt with quickly.

Summing Up the People Part

Although I have presented this information in anecdotal form or in blue jeans as opposed to a suit, this isn't because I feel the information is of casual value. Software development is a human endeavor, the computer is simply a vehicle for implementing our objectives. Because the computer is a nice, predictable machine does not mean that software development is also a nice predictable process. As software development primarily involves people in terms of their wishes, capabilities, and actions, it quickly becomes too complex for any pure formal methodology to define. This isn't to say formal methodologies are bad, as they are about the most powerful tools available to the modern software designer. However, they are tools for controlling the development of the software, for attempting to reduce the unpredictable elements as much as possible. Many people assume that since they are using Yourdon's methodologies or Jackson's or whomever's, then their project is guaranteed to be a success. In such cases the end result is often failure and the participants blame the design methodology, search out a new one, and set themselves up for failure again.

Software development is not a foreseeable process. It is a hideously complex undertaking with a foundation that rests equally in the arts and sciences. As a computer program is unquestionably a sequence of clearly defined logical operations, scientific methods obviously apply. What many do not consider, however, is that there were many ways that these logical sequences we call programs can be written. Science applies to the finished product, defining the hows and whys of its operation. Art applies to the development of the product, biasing many decisions that quantitatively are equal. For this reason, the two standards most experienced programmers apply to any program are:

- Is it elegant?
- Does it work?

Elegance in software is not a trivial concept, it is central to the definition of a good program. A good program has a clearly recognizable structure and every part of the program should work together to emphasize this structure. The fastest way to judge a piece of software is to run it and make a cursory examination of the code. In many cases, you won't have trouble deciding that it's either great or gruesome.

In the rapid prototyping environment, it is especially critical that you pay attention to these issues, more so than in normal environments. In traditional applications, say a customer billing application, it is unlikely that a rapid prototyping approach would be used. The problem is fairly straightforward and the client is incapable of working up much excitement about the issue. In the rapid prototyping environment the issues are more complex, the client is much less sure of exactly what they want, and they tend to generally behave like manic depressives, first operating on the assumption that this new software is going to be the best thing that ever happened to them and then assuming this is the stupidest thing they have ever done.

These meetings are the way you get all of the information you use to develop the software and where all course corrections are made. To do without them or to ignore them means that your development will be uncontrolled.

The Log

As client meetings are the usual location for rapid prototyping, insofar as the software could very likely be modified over lunch in response to an idea that only surfaced that morning, you can see how it is necessary to keep a log about the changes that have been made to the system and the motivations behind these actions.

You cannot simply consider the log as a mere historical record of the system's evolution. You will find yourself referring to it often in order to ensure that the overall development of the system is harmonious so you don't spend this week undoing what you did last week, but instead continue to move forward with development of the system. While the exact format of this log is a decision that will come from within the development group (as opposed to an externally mandated standard), there are certain criteria that it must meet, regardless of the actual format.

The most important thing is that you faithfully maintain it. While there isn't any need to put obvious trivia into it, such as minor changes to some shabby piece of code, if you have any doubts whatever about whether or not something should go into the log, put it in. As you are doing this, make sure you keep an accurate sequence of both dates and version numbers in the log so you know when changes were made and which versions of the system they affected.

In addition to the paper trail created by the log, you should also create an electronic form of the log which at the very least keeps a running copy of the software at each stage of its development. This is extremely important as you will often find it necessary to return to previous versions so you can compare their behavior to the current behavior of the system. As I have stressed, rapid prototyping guarantees you software that is in a permanent state of flux, where the only constant you can depend on is that nothing is constant.

Some Smalltalk platforms, most notably Smalltalk-80 from ParcPlace, come with a very sophisticated change management system. This system tracks all of the changes that have been made to the Smalltalk system, the sum total of which is your software package. In using this system you can rapidly get information on all changes, on changes that affect one or more specific classes, or even changes that took place in a certain order. When dealing with rapid prototyping as a joint effort between multiple programmers, this becomes an extremely important issue, as a fair amount of constant effort must be expended ensuring that all programmers are working from the same basic system. Your progress in rapid prototyping can slow to a crawl if it turns out that all of the project team members are replicating each other's actions because they were either unaware of, or had no access to, the changes made by others.

A tactical detail of some interest in larger rapid prototyping projects involves the appointment of some responsible party to act as the central development coordinator. In groups of three to five people, this is a part-time job that can be done in conjunction with regular development work, but in larger projects it is advisable to make this a full-time responsibility. In any case, the person responsible for change management should also be the one to maintain the paper and electronic logs, as the logs provide the detailed information on the changes being managed.

Summary

In conclusion, I hope you've gotten an idea of the importance of meeting with your clients, so that you can extract information from them, and then ensure that the information you have extracted is both relevant and valid. In the loose arena of RP, these meetings are sometimes the *only* way for you to determine what it is the client expects from you and the system you are developing.

In your meetings with the client you always want to be aware of what kind of meeting you are having, for this defines the agenda. If you are having a strategic meeting of any kind, you are essentially checking to ensure that you and the client share the same conceptual models, and are working towards the same goal. You should walk away from such a meeting with the feeling that you and the client see eye to eye on what you are doing and will do.

When you meet with client staff for informational purposes, you are trying to obtain detailed information to be used in the development of the software. In such meetings, you want to identify those in the client organization that provide the most accurate and timely information, and to avoid like the plague those that provide either completely erroneous information, or put their own "spin" on what would otherwise be useful data. When you leave such a meeting, you should have copious notes and many great ideas of what to do next.

When you meet for large design walkthroughs, you are essentially trying to make sure that the work you have done up to now is correct. These meetings are often quite long and will give you information about the parts of your system that the clients do and do not like. You will also obtain a great deal of information about what they would like to see next, but you should always fix the areas they are unhappy with before proceeding with new development.

- Meetings are not for the purpose of bothering developers, they are an integral part of the development process.
- Meetings are either strategic, which deal with what we are going to do, or tactical, which deal with how to implement our strategic goals.

- Meetings can be held either to obtain detailed information from the client or to ensure that previously extracted information is valid.
- One of RP's great advantages over traditional development methodolgies is that you can react to the clients observations and innuendo much faster, sometimes within the meeting these comments were made.

Exercises

1. If you insist, and have a few cohorts in crime, try to simulate these meetings between yourselves. The most valuable simulation is for the ones pretending to be hostile and combative to clients. This is sometimes the case in the real world, and developers that can handle it have a major advantage over those who can't.

CHAPTER 10

Hard Environmental Issues

Problems worthy of attack prove their worth by hitting back.

Although interpersonal considerations have a definite impact on the prototyping process as shown in Chapter 9, we certainly cannot ignore the role played by the computers that support the prototype. Because software is not developed in a vacuum, but to be integrated with existing electronic and biological systems, we will now redirect our attention to the demands the machine environments place on us.

In Chapter 8, I primarily focused on the fact that we were not implementing the corporate database, rather we were implementing a piece of software expected to interact with the existing corporate database. For this reason we did not have the freedom to define how we would be using the database; this was dictated for us and, in turn, dictated many of our tactical design decisions. We could not force the database to adapt to our design; instead, we were forced to adapt our design to the database. In this chapter I will broaden the scope of those initial observations, dealing with general requirements that apply to all computer-based systems which must be integrated with other existing systems, both computerized and manual. I am focussing on clearly defined systems, those that operate by a known set of rules or procedures, as opposed to more informal systems that operate by consensus or simply by the weight of tradition.

Auditing Requirements

To provide a vehicle for discussing these more general requirements, I will focus on auditing requirements. Auditing of computer software systems, especially those that use or manipulate corporate financial data, is a recognized and well-defined area that covers both computer software and accounting disciplines. Auditing of such information is an easily identifiable concept, for if one were to manage sensitive financial issues without benefit of auditing, one would be asking to be taken to the cleaners by a skilled hacker. Given that the system we are implementing is used to control freight within the Schroeder trucking company, and that the Schroeder Trucking's primary business is the movement of this freight for profit, it is reasonable to assume that we will need to impose or adapt to some form of auditing controls. Given the additional facts that this isn't the first piece of software that the company has purchased and that this software is not responsible for invoicing customers, we can easily determine that, while we will not be required to design and implement new auditing standards, we will be expected to adapt to existing auditing requirements. This is the perfect time to have a quick informational meeting. If we were to find that there was no kind of auditing system in place, we might do well to escalate this issue to a strategic level, informing our client in the strongest possible terms that a formal auditing system should be immediately implemented.

Our first task is to research the current auditing standards. As in any recognized formal system, we can expect to locate one or more documents that define these standards in terms of how they are applied and how they are implemented. Without such information, we would have little chance of successfully adapting our software to meet these requirements. We must hold one or more informational meetings so that we can inform the client personnel of our requirements and allow them to direct us in the appropriate directions. This is a more straightforward process than the extraction of the client's wishes vis à vis the overall operation of the software, in that none of the issues involved are "soft." Instead, we need to know exactly how the auditing system functions and how we are expected to interact with it.

In fact, this is the primary part of our work. Little truly creative work is required, we simply need to know exactly what is expected of us so that we can make our software behave appropriately. For example, if the auditing policy is that no customer shipment is accepted without credit approval, we don't need to do anything fancy. We just need to stop when we have allowed an operator to fill out a complete freight manifest and deliver all of the information we have been given to the auditing system. We don't care how it reaches whatever decision it does reach, we only want to know what that decision is. If it responds that the customer is delinquent and we shouldn't accept the shipment, we discard the data entered by the operator and inform them of this fact. If it approves the new manifest, we just keep going as if nothing had happened.

Much of your work in interfacing with an existing system's requirements is similar to taking a detour when you are driving your car, except in this case you are not required to drive your car through the detour. You can go to sleep when you enter the detour, wake up when you get back on the main road, and check to see whether you have been told to proceed or return to the area from which you came.

For this reason, adapting to requirements imposed by outside systems, electronic or bureaucratic, is usually easier than the identification of the client's desires, which is what we have been doing up to now. In addition, these requirements can usually be satisfied much later in the design process, after we are certain that the software meets the client's requirements. As I have pointed out many times, hard requirements are the easiest to satisfy, for the simple reason that they are the most clearly defined. Therefore, we concentrate our initial efforts on satisfying the soft requirements, assuming that once we have done this we shouldn't have too much trouble solving the hard requirements, such as auditing controls.

Taking an even simpler example, consider the printing of the freight manifests themselves. As the client has been in the business of moving freight around for a while, it isn't too surprising to find that they have been using a standardized waybill for a while, meaning that we can't just go off and decide what the waybill is going to look like when we print it. Instead, we will be expected to take the information we have on file and print it in a specific way on a preprinted form. If this comes as anything of a surprise to you, consider the fact that there are several competing systems out there that handle airline reservations and that airline reservations can be made between almost any two points on the globe. Regardless of what system processed your reservation or printed your tickets, airline tickets all tend to look the same, though they may contain different information. In the same way, we will be expected to fill out the preprinted freight invoices, as opposed to ad-libbing the format.

While on the surface this may appear to be more difficult than designing our own invoice format, actually the reverse is true. Instead of having to use creative thought to design a new form and ensure that all the necessary information is clearly displayed, we simply need to measure the existing form, locating the areas on the form where we will place our information. In the general lingo of software consulting, this is affectionately referred to as a *no-brainer*.

The most important thing to keep in mind when evaluating existing system requirements and adapting the prototype to them is that you should think as little as possible. Your job is not to create anything new, but to ensure that you conform to existing standards. Your only goals should be to seek out the best definition you can find for these standards, to read and understand these definitions, and to ensure that your software is adapted to them. This isn't to imply that anybody can do this, only that you shouldn't spend a great deal of time worrying about whether or not you are doing the right thing. The correct actions will always be defined by the standards and any attempts you make to understand the whys behind these standards will frustrate you and waste your time. Instead, keep your total focus on how you will adapt to these standards.

Interestingly, what I am treating as the more trivial component of the software prototyping process is actually what many have a single-minded focus on. Many existing texts on systems analysis exhort you to seek out such documents, to base your entire design on these documents, and to treat all other inputs from the client as trivial or inconsequential. It is for this reason alone that some software design efforts fail. They have focussed only on the purely mechanical relationships between the new system and the existing systems, totally ignoring the fact that there are end users that have ideas of their own about how the system should behave. If there is one central theme to this book, it is that *the soft issues such as the software's usability and conformance to the client's goals is more important than whether or not the software conforms to existing hard system specifications*. This isn't to say that you can ignore these hard specifications, only that if you create a system which conforms to the end user's goals and the physical system requirements, you will be better off than if you conform only to the physical system requirements. Given that it is much easier to satisfy the clearly defined system requirements than to satisfy the end user's fuzzier hopes and aspirations for the software, you should first determine whether you can make the user happy before you determine whether you can make the other computers happy.

Design Impacts

Having said all this, I don't wish to give you the idea that it is alright to totally ignore these hard requirements. Deciding exactly when and how to pay attention to formal system requirements is a skill that must be honed with practice. The major issue is to determine when each of the formal requirements should be addressed. For certain requirements, such as interfacing with auditing systems, you can often assume that if you are processing a complete set of information, (for example, you aren't missing any of the data that belongs on a waybill) you can defer integration of these requirements until late in the prototyping phase. On the other hand, you will have to deal with some issues earlier, as we saw in the previous chapter on interfacing with the corporate database.

The key difference between these two cases is whether or not the external system has any impact on the fundamental design of the software. In the case of auditing, we already know that the system is processing the data required as input by the auditing system, and we know that the auditing system's primary function is to give us a go/no-go on the various transactions we attempt to perform. We are distantly aware of the fact that the auditing system also keeps an audit trail, but since we are not responsible for maintaining this trail, we can afford to ignore this aspect of the system. This may sound stupid, but many developers get bogged down in attempting to understand aspects of the system that do not directly impact them. This is a serious problem in the RP environment, for the simple reason that you are attempting to quickly react to the client's demands, therefore any time you spend on issues that do not have a direct bearing on your tasks is slowing you down.

Integrating some formal systems, such as the corporate database, has to happen earlier in the design process because these requirements have more dramatic impacts on the design of the prototype itself. Whereas we can view the auditing system as simply something that needs to be "plugged in" to our prototype at the appropriate points, we cannot adopt such a view with the database.

One of the first indicators of this is the fact that interactions with the database can have a definite order to them, an order which is imposed externally on us by the database itself. We cannot decide, for example, to fill out a waybill while leaving the customer information blank, and then fill out the customer information at some other time.

While this may appear to be blatantly obvious, some of the effects are far less obvious. The effects involve the fact that the database itself represents a complex external structure (in terms of the customer data, not the database itself), a structure which is not identical to the structure of our prototype. In short, the information we process within our prototype and in our final system is a subset of all the information the database itself is responsible for supporting. From our viewpoint, the information we are processing is completely integrated, meaning that we have all the necessary pieces and understand how they all fit together. From the perspective of a database system, however, we are in possession of only a small piece of the system, more importantly, one that has connections we are not aware of to elements we are not aware of. For this reason, we must ensure that our prototype behaves the way the database expects it to so that the database may correctly maintain these connections and other elements. Only in doing this can we remain oblivious to the database's external responsibilities.

A good rule of thumb, illustrated by the two preceding cases, is that the more complex the system you must interact with, the earlier you should begin integrating it in the design. The bottom line here is that the auditing system, from our point of view, accepts the information we are processing and tells us whether to continue or halt processing. Therefore we can ignore it until the last part of the prototyping process, or even leave it out of the prototype entirely, as its interaction with our software is minimal. The database, on the other hand, requires us to perform a series of operations in a specific order, which definitely impacts our design. Leaving the database interface totally out of the prototype would most likely be fatal when it came time to produce the final package, for we would have no guarantee that our prototype design would even operate with the database. This isn't to say that we actually have to use the real database, only that we must ensure that our prototype plays by its rules where it expects that of us.

Hardware Requirements

In rapid prototyping, especially when using the Smalltalk language, one pays little attention to the pure hardware requirements that will be imposed on the final software package. I've had one case where a prototype was developed on a Smalltalk platform running on the Apple Macintosh and then ported to FORTRAN running on an IBM 370. Two more different environments would be hard to find. Even so, certain issues were addressed in the prototype because of operating requirements on either the prototype or the target machine.

In dealing with detailed hardware or operational environments imposed by the prototyping or target environment, the very first thing you must make sure to do is to clearly mark them. For example, if you make a decision to accomplish some task in a specific way in the prototype software, although you know that you are doing this primarily for efficiency's sake and will be doing the same thing a completely different way on the target machine, make sure that you clearly call attention to this fact, even if you are the sole member of the team developing the software. For if you do not, the odds are you will forget this in the heat of releasing the final package and will waste a great deal of time looking for some anomaly introduced by this decision. The log I mentioned earlier is invaluable here; this is where the information should be readily available to anyone who needs it. I personally maintain several indices for my development log, one of which specifically deals with such kinds of platform issues. When it comes time for me to construct the final package based on the accepted prototype, the first thing I do is to locate all of these elements and ensure that I don't forget any of them.

Hardware requirements come in two basic flavors: those that deal with the *raw hardware capabilities* of the two platforms and those that deal with the *system environments* on the two platforms. In the area of capabilities, this covers issues such as the presence or absence of specialized hardware such as math co-processing units, the amount of disk storage available for use by the program, connections to the outside world, and so on. The system issues deal with the system's software running on each platform, in terms of what it will and will not allow you to do, and how it expects you to do things.

Some issues are very general, for example whether the system is a graphics-based system like the Macintosh or the Windows environment, or whether it is text-based like the MS-DOS or large time-sharing environment. In cases where the target machine is text-based, Smalltalk is still a good prototyping tool, but there is no point in investing time and effort in sophisticated graphics displays, because the target environment is incapable of supporting such displays. In my own case, I have created a class called CursesPane which implements the standard curses library functions found on many UNIX and MS-DOS environments. This allows me to develop displays on a graphics-based system in such a way that they can be easily moved to a text-based environment because I use a text-based terminology. Although Smalltalk deals with pixels when positioning things on the screen, the CursesPane class allows me to deal with things in terms of character cells and it then deals with moving from the text-based model to the pixel model native to Smalltalk.

Some issues are far more specific, such as whether or not the system has a sophisticated math co-processor. Consider if you were implementing a prototype for a complex engineering system that did a large amount of data analysis, using nasty little things like fourier transforms and power spectrum analysis. On the prototype you might actually have to code up algorithms to accomplish these feats, whereas on the target machine you might be able to access a sophisticated Digital Signal Processor (DSP) chip that already knows how to perform such functions, or you might be required to use some preexisting common library.

The most important task in minimizing the impact of differences between the prototype and target machines, including both hardware and software differences, is to try to define a common ground between the two machines, albeit one biased more towards efficiency on the target platform than on the prototyping platform. After you have identified what is common to both machines, you should identify those things that are dissimilar between the two platforms, placing strong emphasis on making the prototype conform to the target platform. The idea is that you want to make your prototyping environment adapt to the target environment, rather than destroy the efficiency of your target environment by forcing it to adapt to the prototyping environment.

In doing this, you will be constructing a new kind of class, one that I call the glue class for want of a better name. These glue classes, such as the CursesPane class, are classes that implement functions required on the prototype but not on the target and are not really part of either application. Instead, they are environmental details used to mesh the prototype and target environments together. You will find that over time you will have a constantly growing collection of such classes. This will lead to a steady improvement in your ability to adapt to strange target environments by allowing you to manage projects with increasing differences between the target and prototype machines. While some classes are created to satisfy general programming requirements, and some classes such as the Freight class are created to satisfy specific application requirements, the glue classes satisfy rapid prototyping requirements. These glue classes are the main asset of RP specialists, as the more glue classes a rapid prototyper has available to them, the more rapidly they can deal with specific platform issues. These classes are always found in a cross-platform developer's bag of tricks, and rarely in other OOP programmer's bags because as they have no need for them.

Design Structure and Porting

One final issue that relates to machine-specific RP requirements deals with the OOP environment itself and is clearly manifested when one is developing under an OOP environment such as Smalltalk and porting to a non-OOP system such as C or Pascal.

The Smalltalk language operates under the valid assumption that everything it encounters is an object and that all objects are capable of identifying themselves and responding to messages. When porting a Smalltalk prototype to another language, one of these critical assumptions may cause a great deal of trouble in the porting process. Specifically, Smalltalk is a loosely typed system, meaning that it makes determinations as to the specific type of a piece of data at runtime. In Smalltalk, everything is just an object and it is the runtime system's responsibility for determining just what kind of object something is.

This provides you with the ability to construct heterogeneous collections (collections of objects of many different types). This approach is so flexible that you may not even know at compile time exactly what types of objects will be placed into this collection, instead you will depend on the runtime system to dynamically determine the type of each object as it accesses the collection.

Consider a small drawing program, where there is a collection called stuffToDraw. If we simply assume that any object placed into this collection responds to the draw message, then the following code fragment would suffice to draw all of the items in the collection:

```
stuffToDraw do: [:anItem |
    anItem draw].
```

While the ability to do this in Smalltalk is one of the main contributors to the speed in which programs may be implemented, too much dependance on this facility can hinder you when you begin to port the program to a language such as C. The reason for this is due to the fact that C is, at least compared to Smalltalk, a strongly typed system—meaning that it expects you to declare the exact type of each variable you define in your code, because it cannot determine the type of the variable at runtime. This means that you can run into serious problems when you expect the runtime system to sort out all of the type-sensitive operations by dynamically checking the type of each object as it processes it.

I will deal with this subject in far more detail in Chapter 13, specifically ways in which you can move a loosely typed prototype into a strongly typed environment. For now, I want to concentrate on the fact that you should recognize when there are certain fundamental structural differences between your prototyping system and the final target system. Although it is not impossible to implement what looks like a loosely typed model in a strongly typed system, it does require that you provide a fair amount of underlying code to support this dynamic determination of type.

For this reason, you should always be sensitive to the fact that one of the great speed advantages provided by many rapid prototyping environments, especially those using Smalltalk, is based on the fact that it takes a lot less work to ignore static type declarations when you are writing the code and simply let the runtime system figure it all out when it's necessary. In short, it is hard to waste a lot of time resolving variable type conflicts when the language doesn't even pay attention to types in the first place. However, wanton abuse of this privilege can produce designs so dependant on a loose typing model that they can never be successfully moved to a strongly typed environment.

In saying this, I don't want to make you feel as though you should avoid the use of loose typing, especially in the context of collections and parameters to methods. I simply want you to always remain cognizant of the fact that you are expecting the computer to do part of your job for you, and that you will pay a price for this. Foremost, since the computer dynamically determines the type of each object as it encounters it, rather than doing this job once at compile time, your code will be a lot less efficient. Secondly, since the computer is allowing you to ignore typing as you write the code, which in turn will serve as the specification for the final software package, use the log to keep track of what type or types you expect the real system to encounter. This information will be invaluable to you when you go to port the software to the target machine.

Let's examine the first issue in more detail. It means you should always factor this inherent inefficiency in when you are determining the optimum algorithm to use in solving a particular problem. In most cases, selection of specific processing algorithms can safely be deferred to the final port, and the easiest coded algorithms can be used in the prototype. If there are multiple competing algorithms and they all accept exactly the same parameters and produce exactly the same results, I don't recommend you waste your time selecting the most efficient one during prototyping. Just pick the one that's already in the class hierarchy or the easiest one to enter into the hierarchy and leave it at that. Selection of the optimum algorithm in this case is a job best left for the final porting phase. On the other hand, if you are exploring competing algorithms that have notable interface differences, you should attempt to discriminate between speed issues that are directly related to the structure of the algorithm as opposed to those issues related to the overhead which occurs in a loosely typed system.

As the idea in rapid prototyping is to quickly produce and modify a running program, the less type declarations wired into the code, the better. The most obvious advantage is the simple fact that you aren't sitting around scratching your head and wondering what type you should assign to each variable you create. Subtler, but no less important differences arise when you begin to modify this code. When you modify the code you don't have to worry about modifying your variable types, as it doesn't matter much to the system, as long as they understand the messages they receive. So this saves you a lot of time, allowing you to quickly modify the system without worrying about type clashes.

As long as you are aware of the fundamental difference between a strongly typed system that requires you to explicitly declare the class or type of each variable at compilation time and a loosely typed system that figures out these details at runtime, you shouldn't have any major problems. But if you depend too much on this and create designs that depend on the fact that the runtime system will sort out all of your typing for you, you could be forced to either change a great deal of your design during the port or to introduce a lot of inefficiencies by duplicating loose typing in your final port. Be careful. Loose typing is a very powerful tool in the rapid prototyping environment, but like any powerful tool, it will hurt you if you misuse it.

Summary

As you are seeing, the harder issues enter into the prototyping process after much of the fundamental system concepts and behaviors have been worked out. Some issues, such as integration with external systems like database managers, need to be done before the prototype gets to the point where it wants to perform detailed tasks that conflict with these external systems, as we saw in Chapter 7.

Some issues, however, can be ignored up until the end of the RP cycle, or even ignored until the final port of the system. When you are dealing with external systems such as an auditing package, you are usually expected to give it the data you have available, and wait for it to tell you whether or not you can continue. Given that this system is both rigidly defined, and simply acts as a switch on your own logic, you don't need to worry too much about it.

In fact, worrying about it can cause you problems. In cases such as this, you don't want to be creative, you simply want to link the systems together at the appropriate point and put in a branch that is driven by the response from this external system. You don't need to make far-ranging changes to you prototype in such cases. You are, more often than not, dealing with something that is effectively saying "keep going" or "return to your starting point."

Equally important are environmental issues involving the final target machines for your software. These issues don't have specific effects on your design, instead they have subtle long-term impacts on the decisions you make throughout your design process. The best way to deal with these kinds of issues is to have a conceptual understanding of the difference between the machine and environment you are developing the prototype on and the machine and environment the final application will run on. With such an understanding, you have the information necessary to guide you through the RP cycle.

In conclusion, these kinds of environmental issues have no directly visible impact on the logic of the system in the way that the database system does. In the first case, the interface is fairly trivial, and the auditing system is clearly defined. It is open to argument whether or not you even need to deal with it in the prototype. In many cases you will find that the decision to implement auditing in the prototype would have more political than technical overtones. In dealing with cross-platform hard issues, these are very subtle effects, once again not resulting in much code that you can point to and say, "See, there's the effect."

- Don't over analyze rigidly defined external systems. Such systems expect you to follow rules, they don't like it if you try to be creative.
- There is a big difference between integrating with a system such as a database, where we are effectively doing a job for it, and integrating with an audit trail manager, where it is doing a job for us.
- Know your platforms. This means both the language, the operating system, and the hardware.
- Keep platform differences in mind. Don't do things in the prototype that would cause the target platform to gag.
- Identify glue classes and keep them in your bag of tricks. The best way to avoid platform conflicts is to establish a *virtual* platform based on the shared capabilities of both.

Exercises

1. Develop a toy application, such as a temperature converter under Smalltalk. Assume your target platform is assembly language on the prototype system, but you aren't allowed to use the operating system. Identify design decisions that would cause you pain.

2. If you have access to more than one platform, try to define a virtual development platform that covers them all. Identify the *glue* classes you would need to implement.

3. If you are a masochist, try something like this: create a fancy pixel-based window under Smalltalk on a Macintosh, using all the fancy bits of the Mac interface. The window should do some kind of string art like many demo programs. Now port this application to a DOS machine with a text-based display, using a language like ADA. After you finish this, you should be quite sensitive to cross-platform issues.

CHAPTER 11

Iteration in Rapid Prototyping

He who lives by the crystal ball soon learns to eat ground glass.

I have addressed the individual elements of the standard rapid prototyping environment, using the approach of what the computers and humans you interact with will expect from you and be able to provide to you. In this chapter, I would like to deal with the circular nature of this process, illustrating how it is not so much a linear progression from start to finish, but instead a process that repeats until a valid reason is found for stopping it.

The best illustration of this is anecdotal and comes from the first project I ever used these techniques in, before I even knew that the rapid prototyping concept existed. It wasn't until later that year at the OOPSLA conference, an annual conference on object-oriented programming, that I saw a presentation from the Xerox Special Information Systems group and actually heard the term *rapid prototyping*. I was amazed to find that all these great new discoveries of mine were not so new, but I was pleased to find that others had also been successful with the approach.

I was developing a window-based replacement for a rather clumsy command-line oriented communications package and I decided to use Smalltalk to design the user interface. After initial hesitancy from the clients, they decided they liked the approach, especially the fact that we could rapidly change and reconfigure the user interface once they had the opportunity to interact with it. As I've stated, this approach allowed us to work out together what their desired interface looked like, through a trial and error process, rather than attempting to divine all of the characteristics of the interface from the very beginning. We constantly repeated the steps I've described up to now, changing and fine-tuning the interface for several months. Finally, there came a point where the decision was made, "That's it. That's exactly what we want. Just make it go faster!" We ported the entire Smalltalk package to the Microsoft Windows environment, version 1.03, in a month and a half of my time. I had never even used Windows before, and 1.03 had a widely known reputation for being a breeding ground for bugs. Having the Smalltalk program as a working specification allowed us to easily circumvent all of the bugs without loosing sight of our end objective.

Iteration in the Rapid Prototyping Design Cycle

You are probably already familiar with the standard *edit->compile->test* loop that most programmers spend their time in. You write code, fiddle with it until the compiler likes it, and then try to run it, which leads you quickly back to the edit cycle. At some point you expect to actually break through the test cycle into the land of released software, but we all know this really means that you just start all over again on the next version. A simple fact of life in the programming environment is that code is not immutable, instead it has an evolutionary inertia. That inertia is only overcome at some point by the prohibitive cost of modifications to a program that can now be most clearly described as patches on top of patches.

By being aware of the differences between OO programs and traditional programs, and by exploiting your knowledge of these differences, you will be able to deal with this process more naturally, tightly coupling the tactical changes in the program that affect its technical characteristics with the strategic changes to the program that affect how it interacts with the user and its environment.

As I said in Chapter 1, software design is changing, primarily because we've solved the easier problems. The stock applications, such as traditional business software, have been implemented so many times that they are now commodity products, as opposed to ones containing any kind of new technology. Therefore, the applications we are now writing are more complex, pushing the fringes of what we know about the design of software. This isn't only happening in the software environment, there is much being done in hardware also, especially in such areas as massively parallel computers. This too affects the software we are writing, by changing some of our basic assumptions concerning the platforms our software will run on.

The *ostrich* approach, favored for some time in software engineering, is in essence based on the statement that clients give fuzzy designs because they are too lazy to give completely specified designs. Nothing could be further from the truth. Clients give fuzzy designs because they expect to get feedback on them. They expect to work with software developers and the software itself, helping to identify the route that the software will follow in its evolution from an idea to a released package. This constant feedback is vital to the process, but there is also no question that it conflicts with traditional environments where the investment in constructing a program precludes arbitrary changes that might "break" it.

OO programming, with its focus on small interconnected modules, allows one to deal with the situation in a realistic manner. By first recognizing that software is always, to one extent or another, in a state of flux, we can begin to examine how our development environment can deal with this. We need to identify what pieces of our applications are or are not opposed to change, and how the tools we use to implement our software help or hinder this process.

OO design is built around the concept of classes, which helps us to naturally divide our programs into their constituent components and deal with each of the components as a stand-alone unit. In doing this, we can entertain change requests to a particular component, or class, knowing that the changes we make will be confined to this class, with minimal intrusion into other classes. This means we never look at changes to a basic component with the sinking feeling that to change one little thing, we'll have to change everything.

Architectural Issues

However, no program is built around the concept of classes. Instead, it is built around the concept the application is meant to implement. The application's overall design is not subservient to the computer's wishes, it's subservient to the end user's wishes. This isn't to say you should totally ignore the requirements imposed by the computer, only that your job as a developer is to have the computer implement the user's wishes, not the other way around.

For this reason, there are certain areas of your design that are less amenable to change than others, but these areas involve the core architecture of the program, as opposed to the details of its operation. In our case study of Schroeder Trucking, the basic concept of a multi-window display system supporting the point and click navigational model is a core architectural decision, and would therefore be difficult to modify after we were deep in the prototyping process. On the other hand, details about exactly what it is that we present in each of these windows and the whys and hows of navigation between the windows are much easier to change.

In developing an object-oriented program in a rapid prototyping environment, you must clearly separate these two parts of the design. Until you have clearly defined the architecture, you can't even begin the prototyping process. You don't have to have hideously formal architectural specification, but you should know the basic objectives of the system and how it will be expected to interact with the users and the systems around it. This information, in turn, will tell you a great deal about the application classes that will be necessary to implement your design. This is, however, another indicator of the inflexibility of the underlying architecture, in that it dictates many of your application class requirements. Change the architecture and you change many of the application class requirements.

Architectural issues are technical design issues, insofar as they deal with how a particular application is to be implemented on a target platform. However, the driving force behind these issues is not the platform, but the user community. For this reason, you do not define the architecture in terms of what the computer can do, instead, you define the architecture in terms of what the users wish to do, limiting these wishes when it is obvious that the platform is not going to cooperate. This is really the only contribution of the platform at this time, to limit what can be done.

For example, if a user was requesting a voice command system for the Schroeder Trucking application, we would probably override this because the platform simply isn't powerful enough to support such a task. But we aren't using the platform to say what the architecture should be, only to determine the things that *absolutely cannot be done*. You don't want to confuse what is difficult with what is impossible, for you should make every effort not to let the difficulty of implementation bias your architectural decisions. Apple Macintosh and Microsoft Windows code is more difficult to write than traditional computer software; however, the architectural benefits far outweigh the difficulty in implementation. Remember, the architecture of the software has a lot to do with its look and feel and with its core operational characteristics. You want the architecture to be as natural as possible, so your objective in examining it from the machine's perspective is only to determine whether or not something is possible.

You shouldn't blindly ignore feasibility issues throughout the design process. You simply want to delay discussing issues based on feasibility until you have constructed an architectural structure that defines the system, one on which you will hang its components. Issues of feasibility are not truly involved with the architectural description; they are attached to the construction of the components that will implement the architecture. It may become apparent that the architecture will have to be modified to account for feasibility issues, but this should only be done in concert with a defined architecture. In other words, feasibility issues involve modifications to an existing architecture, whereas platform capability issues involve the architecture itself. The feasibility issues address the difficulty of a task, whereas platform capabilities address whether a task is possible.

The construction of the final architecture involves the formation of a concept, followed by determining if the concept is possible, followed by determining if the concept is practical. At each stage of the design you may find yourself returning to a previous phase, with effects ranging from slight tweaks to enhance performance to trashing the entire design and starting over.

Implementation Issues

Implementation issues are those that deal strictly with implementing a specified architecture. Platform capability issues rarely arise here, but if they do the only true solution is to rework the architecture until they go away. In doing this, you may effectively render all of your efforts up to now invalid in the new architecture. As this event happens to the best of us, I can only say that you should realize that this will be one of the most difficult parts of rapid prototyping—you rest easy knowing it only happens rarely.

If you do find yourself dealing with major architectural revisions, you will probably want to keep your current work in mind so that your changes to the architecture don't invalidate all of your existing implementation classes. I can only stress that you should remember that this is an artificial action, and is not really supposed to affect architectural decisions. In the real world, given the cost of developing software, you will be forced by external considerations to attempt to salvage your current work. You must also remember that this action is automatically endangering the new architecture by grossly limiting its scope. If, for example, you had already implemented a set of file management classes and were loathe to discard them, you have effectively limited your architecture to these features, whenever the architecture needs to connect to the file system. You should also remember that within the application classes you have developed so far are the parts that caused the initial architecture. They are invaluable in generating new architecture and dangerous in that they can easily infect the new architecture with the same logic disease that killed its predecessor.

Happily, most implementation issues deal primarily with implementing specific classes to solve architectural requirements. This is the process I illustrated earlier when we designed a portion of the freight management software. This process is much longer that the example given in the book, but it is done in increments even smaller than the one we originally showed. In a system capable of supporting rapid prototyping, you will usually find yourself making a small set of revisions to a few classes and then testing the application again. In a traditional system, application downtime (the time the application source files are in flux and cannot be used to generate the application because of source file or linkage errors) can easily be a week or more. Smalltalk applications are usually never "non-functional," they usually just have some sections that are fully built and finished, whereas other sections can leave you clinging to an architectural beam. As the environment is totally integrated, with the entire library update process managed automatically by the system itself, the average edit->compile->test cycle in Smalltalk rarely runs over an hour or so.

This is one of the primary reasons I have stressed interaction with the software and the user community. Rapid prototyping ensures that you can do daily demos of the software, showing its incremental growth in capabilities over time. As the individual changes are all quite small and are automatically integrated into the overall system, you are following more of an evolutionary design path than you are a traditional structured design path. In fact, the output from the RP design cycle is a program, which serves as a formal structured specification for implementing the real system on its target platform.

You will often find yourself asking, "What do I do next?" during the rapid prototyping process because you don't have a detailed map telling you where to go. You have the architecture and you know that you must continue to add components into it until it's fully fleshed out, at which time you will have finished. In the early stages you will often find yourself overwhelmed by the choices open to you.

You should always bias your decisions towards those that produce the most visible effects, until you are positive that the architecture for the new system satisfies your clients. If you fail to do this, then you risk delivering something they don't want. So develop a rough model of the front end first, and get the clients to interact with it. Then work with the clients, pushing the functionality through so that the system behaves as they expect it to.

As this process unfolds, you will repeat this *edit->demo* cycle automatically. I oppose this to the edit->compile->test cycle deliberately, to stress the fact that compiles and links are handled immediately at the conclusion of the edit cycle by the editor and that since the prototype is more or less operational, demos are almost constantly possible. Testing can be seen as a process of demonstrating the software to yourself and altering areas where the actual behavior of the prototype does not match your mental model of that prototype's behavior. You should always seek to augment this process, especially when you are unsure of what to do next, or are at a stage when a certain behavior of the system needs to be signed off on by the user community.

Binding Assumptions

In developing any system in a rapid prototyping environment, you must be sensitive to issues that imply certain capabilities of *all* platforms your design will be run on, in both prototype and final forms. The platform definition encompasses the hardware of the physical platform and the language system that will be used to generate or operate the prototype or final package.

Object-Oriented Platform Ports

I have referred to the strong typing/weak typing issue several times, as an example of the fundamental differences between object-oriented language implementations. In a weakly or loosely typed system such as Smalltalk, the system doesn't keep track of the types of any individual object, instead it simply queries an object about the object's type when it needs this information. This allows you to easily construct such things as *heterogeneous* collections, collections which contain all sorts of different kinds of objects. In our case study, we might implement an instance of Collection called todaysTransactions, into which we throw every freight manifest, change order, and financial transaction we process. At the end of the day we can dump out this collection and sort it into its constituent parts.

In strongly typed languages such as C++ you must define the exact class of the objects you place into a collection. While it is possible to generalize and say you are building a collection of Objects, assuming that all the elements you wished to put in it were derived from Object, you are still confronted by a serious problem. One of the main reasons that a language is strongly typed is so the compiler can efficiently generate code, and there is a level of syntactical error checking when the code is compiled. However, the compiler discards most of this information when the program is compiled, as it feels this information has been hardwired into the object program it created.

This means that, although you can cast a derived class to its base class type and back again, you can't get any help from the machine because it doesn't actually know the class type of any object. In our previous example, we would have to provide some mechanism that can identify the type of each transaction objects in the collection.

Weak typing is necessary for RP because it allows you to create and change programs rapidly without worrying about *type clash* issues. The only kind of type conflict you can have in such a system is a particular piece of code's assumption that an object will respond to a particular message. As most changes involve extending the hierarchy, which maintains the chain of method inheritance, changes in one area usually don't affect other areas. The two most common ways of getting this message is either to delete a class that is being used in the application or move the class to some remote area of the hierarchy.

For this reason, you will depend on the ability of a loosely-typed system. In most cases, this supports easy modification of parameters and limited use of heterogeneous collections. What you should not encounter is the extensive use of heterogeneous collections that can carry many distinct types. You will find many collections that manage between one and four distinct data types. These collections are normal and pose no portability issues. If, on the other hand, you find a collection into which you are dumping 10 or more different kinds of objects and worse yet, this capability is a central part of your design, you may have a serious portability problem. In such a case, your design depends on loose typing and to change this dependance you would have to alter the design radically. This problem may be circumvented, but with a definite cost, as I shall explain in future chapters. As far as the former type of collections, those containing a few number of classes, are concerned, they can be modified to use different methods and subcollections to keep the data separated internally. This entire process would be transparent to users.

I'm not trying to say you can never use loose typing in your design, only that it has serious performance impacts. In some cases you will find the only way to solve a problem properly requires that you use loose typing in the final product, but this means you will have to duplicate in the final version those parts of the prototyping environment that support loose typing. This is a subtle issue to new developers because they aren't yet comfortable with the fact that decisions can be made for them without their explicit commands. You must always be aware of this in prototyping environments—the fact that, without your attention, you may find the design depending on features of the prototyping environment itself. When this happens, you will always have two choices open to you: to hack the design and remove the dependency or to duplicate the prototype environment capabilities on the target platform. These are not the most pleasant choices one could make, especially if the entire problem has come as a nasty Monday morning present.

Non-Object-Oriented Platform Ports

In porting an application prototyped in Smalltalk or another OOL to a non-OOL, you are going to be dealing with the fact that your entire program assumes there is such a thing as an object, whereas the target platform is oblivious to objects. Not only do you have to move from one language to another, you must also globally change a central paradigm within the software.

Although this may appear to be a daunting process, it isn't too bad if you examine the requirements closely. Regardless of whether you are porting a Smalltalk program to an OOL such as C++, or to a non-OOL such as C, you are going to be rewriting every line of source. Admittedly, this is a fairly simple translation exercise in the first case and has even been automated to some extent. The basic fact remains that in a port from one language to another, you are going to read every line of code at least once even if you have automated tools helping you out.

In porting to a non-OOL, you will also need to read through the code, but this time you will have to convert from the object paradigm to the paradigm of the language you are using. In doing this, you have two choices. You can construct a general toolkit that implements object-oriented system facilities and then build your object-oriented program on top of this, or you can rewrite the original object-oriented program in the target language.

Adding Object-Oriented Capabilities

One avenue open to you is to create a toolkit of functions that allow you to support the concept of objects and message passing. In many higher-level languages, you can implement structures that are like objects, but which don't have any methods. *Message passing* is essentially a function lookup process, where one uses some type of key to look up a function address in a table. By embedding some typing information in each structure and creating dispatch functions for each of your classes to support the message passing, you can allow object-oriented programs to be implemented in your final language. (This is not a trivial exercise, but there are packages available for languages such as C, Pascal, and LISP that provide the necessary facilities.)

The advantage to this approach is that once you have done this, you have drastically reduced the work required to port future prototypes to this same environment. The cost to you has been in two areas. First, you may have invested a substantial amount of time in the process of creating this library of common OOP functions. Secondly, laying this extra layer into the running system will introduce some performance penalties, but these can be controlled with judicious programming.

If you are porting a single application to a single environment, and never expect to port another application or modify the original application, you can ignore implementing an OOP function library, but in any other case you would be well advised to implement and use such a function library. You would reach programming perfection when the hierarchy of your prototyping environment meshed seamlessly with the OO function library on the target machine, as your ports would then essentially become automatic translation exercises.

Hardcoding the System

You can forgo the implementation of a OO function library, which means that you are treating the Smalltalk program as a final specification for implementing the application on the target machine. This is a vast improvement over other kinds of specifications for the simple reason that you know that it is logical and reflects exactly what the user is expecting to receive.

Analysis of port time and material constraints follow traditional analysis procedures at this point, with the Smalltalk source code serving as the primary working document. The development process would be traditional modular implementation, aided by the fact that object-oriented programs already are naturally divided into appropriate modules. The basic truth at this point is that you have an excellent specification for development in a traditional environment. You should seriously consider collecting development metrics during this process, because you will find their granularity is small enough, given the object decomposition already performed, that they allow you to make excellent projections of future tasks of this type. I use the Construction Cost Model (COCOMO) and I can quickly estimate a new project based on the metrics I have collected to a very small degree of error (less than 10 percent usually).

The biggest chance you take is if you revise the prototype. Revision of the prototype is equivalent in this case to revision of a detailed development plan. In most cases, given that the revisions to the prototype are simple, the corresponding revisions to the final system should also be simple. Unfortunately, there will be cases where what appears to be a very simple change in the object-oriented paradigm will have far-reaching effects in the final implementation, forcing you to restart or extensively modify the development plan. Also, if you make changes to the development plan without modifying the prototype itself, you can get out of sync with your specification.

You should only use such an approach when you have no choice and at least two of the following reasons are valid:

- Your choice of an implementation language is tightly constrained.
- You are never going to change the prototype again.

- The final implementation is going to be an exact copy of the prototype, functionally speaking.
- You have very serious space or speed considerations.

Graphics Issues

Smalltalk is unquestionably built around a graphical user interface (GUI) and any user interface developed in this environment is going to reflect this bias towards a GUI. If you expect to be porting to a text-oriented system, you will probably want to subclass pane and create a terminal emulator pane, one that you can use to model all of the cursor movement and editing commands that the target terminal understands. If you then build your interface on top of this class, you shouldn't find any portability problems (as long as you realize the final interface is going to be more primitive than what could be accomplished, given the features available to you).

This is a reasonable approach that I've used successfully. I once wrote a Smalltalk program for a client that allowed a user to interactively design windows and menus that were run in text mode on an IBM-PC. The final window library came from Vermont Creative Software (Windows for C/Windows for Data) and the Smalltalk design system was built on top of a PureTextPane class. By implementing methods that mimicked the VCS operations, we made a fancy GUI running on an EGA display allowing us to develop brain-dead text interfaces.

The one thing you don't want to do is to implement user interfaces that you can't duplicate on your target machine. This would lead to serious design revisions that could ruin you. If you have been aware of platform limitations when crafting the initial architecture, this should never happen to you.

In porting between two GUI's, you can depend on the fact that most, if not all GUI's are related to Smalltalk. Both Microsoft Windows and the Macintosh toolbox provide facilities that are quite similar to the facilities provided by the Smalltalk environment. This means that most of your interface should port directly between these two platforms and have the same look and feel across all platforms.

In these environments, there is always a common denominator you can depend on. All graphics operations are carried out by a single function, known as bitblt (bitblit), which is a function that performs bit block transfers, the operations that actually move the bits around to create the display. By examining the Smalltalk class hierarchy, you can see that all graphics display operations, from the simple to the sublime, eventually trigger a series of bitblt operations to do their work. For this reason, if you find yourself in need of a GUI facility, such as pull-down menus, that is unusable in the target platform, you can implement them by identifying the bitblt operations in Smalltalk and reimplementing them in the target environment.

Summary

RP is much like traditional development in that it is an iterative process that you repeat until you have the product you want, or you run out of time to continue fiddling with the software. The primary difference arises from the fact that in OO development, the cycle is much shorter and therefore occurs much more often.

This is exactly what makes OO systems so useful in the RP environment. Since the cycle is so much faster, you don't need as detailed a road map as you do in traditional design. Feedback works well when it can act quickly upon the system it is controlling, but not so well when its effects are delayed by weeks or months. Because OO systems are broken apart into smaller modules, and because the systems support a large part of the mechanical details of system assembly, you get feedback about design decisions in hours, or days at the most. This means that when your feedback tells you that you have done something bad, you haven't invested so much in it that you are forced to live with it.

You do need to be aware of what is and is not easy to modify in the RP environment. Issues involved with the core behavior of the system, the behavior that governs the system's basic look and feel, is no easier to change in the RP environment than it is in any other environment. The primary ability to change within an RP environment rests on the fact that the program is composed of a large number of small interconnected modules. Any of these modules can be changed easily, but the core architecture has affected how all of the modules were constructed, therefore changes to the core architecture imply changes to many of the modules in the system.

In the RP development cycle, you do need to be aware of certain platform characteristics that you are depending on to support you, such as loose typing. You need to use loose typing in the RP development cycle, because it allows you to easily change the linkages between objects without worrying about type clashes and similar problems. On the other hand, you want to be sure that if your final target environment is not amenable to loose typing that this is all you use loose typing for. If you were to go farther and use loose typing to support such things as heterogeneous collections, you would be forced to change all of this when porting the software to the final environment.

- RP, like all program development, is iterative. The big difference is that the cycle is much faster.
- Changes to independent issues, such as the behavior of a particular component, are easy.
- Changes to interdependent issues, such as the basic architecture of the system, are far more difficult because many elements of the system are impacted by the change.
- You should identify things that cannot be done on a platform and inform a client accordingly. This means you can tell them they can't do real time animation on a circa 1981 IBM PC.
- You should not tell clients they can't do things because they are difficult. You can't do things that are impossible; difficult is not equal to impossible.

- RP depends on loose typing, but your design doesn't have to. Using loose typing for RP doesn't mean the target platform has to support it, but using loose typing in your design means the target platform must support it or your design must change.

- If you are moving a program developed on an OO platform to a non-OO platform, be aware that you will either have to switch the structure to a straight procedural framework or implement a function library to support OO operations.

- If the target can't do something, don't do it in the prototype just because it's there. If the target uses glass TTYs, then don't do fancy styled text in the prototype interface.

CHAPTER 12

Reverse Engineering

Understanding the laws of nature does not mean that we are free from obeying them.

Finally, the time comes when one must freeze the prototyping process and get on with the job of implementing the target system version. I have been mentioning areas that concern this happy event in previous chapters, areas involving what thou shalt and shalt not do in developing the prototype regarding target platform portability issues. This event is unquestionably a major milestone in the project's lifecycle and many things change.

To the relief of many, the project will now become manageable using traditional development techniques, such as those presented by Yourdon and Jackson. While these traditional methods haven't been used up to now, it was only because the starting point was so vague and we had no way of satisfying their front end requirements. Now that we are in possession of a working prototype and the software that implements it, we are in a better position to comply with the requirements of formal development methods.

Getting the Client to Sign Off

This may sound like a silly issue, but it isn't. With the highly interactive nature of the rapid prototyping development process and the degree to which the client is able to interact with it, the client easily becomes hooked on this, especially if they have been abused during previous development efforts. The client is now able to give input about anything from the choice of text fonts to the core control flow of the system, and to actually see results in hours or days.

Given that this can be a new experience for many clients, they will often revel in the process. The developers, for a combination of monetary and intellectual reasons, are usually glad to indulge them, and we end up with a situation where nobody is watching the clock.

Many RP projects will stay in the prototype revision stage until the client spends all their money. This isn't funny, it's true. I have been involved in three separate projects where this happened. I've never seen any bad feelings engendered, instead their has always been this agreement between the clients and the developers that it was a lot of fun and isn't this one slick piece of software. Unfortunately for the clients, they now have to go to their management and explain that they were having so much fun that they lost track of expenses.

In these cases, more money was made available to perform the final system port and there was a high degree of enthusiasm and trust. The only change was that the clients finally stopped fiddling with the prototype and you could move it to the target machine.

As a rapid prototyper you should watch for the point where the client begins to concentrate on exclusively cosmetic changes. Somewhere after this point, they will begin to waste a lot of time switching back and forth between things that have been tried before, rather than contributing any new concepts. This is not to say that cosmetic issues are unimportant, only that in time they will degenerate into an argument about whether a control should be blue or green.

As you can see from Figure 12-1, you can easily get stuck in a perpetual loop when various competing factions attempt to diverge from the group consensus. Your job is to identify when the group's cosmetic details have been satisfied and then jump around the squabbling to the development of the target system. While this activity is often a source of profits to any contractors involved, it produces more smoke than heat and should be avoided by reputable designers.

Figure 12-1: The endless loop.

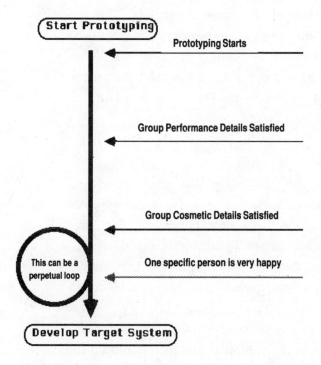

When the client signs off on the prototype, it should be explained to them that it wouldn't be a good idea to attempt more changes in the prototype. It would be nice to categorically forbid them from changing the prototype, but there is always a chance that they are going to have to make a necessary and important modification to the prototype. The developer's job is to identify what is truly necessary.

Before you commence implementing the final system, you must be certain that the client understands that this is a major milestone and the specification for the prototype is the only thing that passes on to the next phase. They must understand that any future changes will cause us to return to this side of the milestone because we can't just dump new ideas into the implementation specification. This specification is produced from the prototype and whenever the prototype changes, it must be regenerated. Changes to the prototype while the final system is being developed should be frowned upon.

The goal is to have the client say that the prototype reflects their exact wishes and they want it to run the same way on the final platform, although they might wish it ran a little faster. This statement, formalized in a memorandum represents the sign off process and allows you to proceed with the next step of development.

Extracting the Specifications

You are now in possession of the four things you need in order to write the implementation specifications. You have the working prototype; the Smalltalk source code for this prototype; the log you have painstakingly maintained, which carries all of the design decisions, notes on implementation issues, and the set of manuals to the external systems you must use; and the target environment you will be developing and running in.

The most important piece is the source listing of all the classes you used in the prototype. I stress "used" because this listing should include not only those classes you actually created for the prototype, but also all classes you used from the system hierarchy. Keep these lists separated, because the former are for this application alone, while the latter are for all future projects.

The first step is to produce a good listing of the Smalltalk classes used in the prototype. I use Microsoft Word and extensively format the listings so that my classes come out looking like this:

Object subclass: #Freight

instanceVariableNames:
```
    waybill
    origin
    destination
    location
    nextIntermediateDestinations
    prevIntermediateDestinations
    customer
    priority
    dateReceived
    dateDue
    timeDue
```
classVariableNames:
```
    MasterManifestLog
    WaybillCounter
```
poolDictionaries: <none>

Freight class methods

```
new
    ^super new initialize
```

Freight instance methods

```
customer
    ^customer!
```

As you know, this class contains more code than shown here, but the fragment shows a possible way of formatting the information.

In addition to formatting, you can never have too many cross indices. You should create cross indices that will show you which classes use and are used by which classes, which methods in a class modify a certain class or instance variable, and all the other little details about interactions between the classes. You will find that while the nicely formatted code shows you how a particular method accomplishes a task, it is the cross indices that show how the various classes of the system work together to implement the application.

Writing the Specifications

With a notebook containing the formatted cross-indexed source to the prototype, the analysis documents we produced when writing the prototype, and the running prototype, you have enough information to write specifications. As you have already used the rapid prototyping process to consolidate a large number of vague ideas into a single clearly defined concept, you can proceed with the assurance that you can provide the necessary amount of detail to survive in this process.

The Requirements Document

The first step is to generate the requirements document, which is supposed to define the exact requirements of the software we are to implement. This document will be a detailed description of the prototype, in terms of its behavior as perceived by a user. The actual code is not of interest here; instead, we are concentrating on defining exactly how the prototype operates and the tasks that it performs. Our real requirement is to duplicate the prototype on a new platform, so it follows that the functional requirements are simply an exact description of the prototype's behavior. This is a far cry from the more common process of defining functional requirements, which involves starting at the same point as the prototyping process and then immediately writing the requirements by pretending that the client already has a clear grasp on what they want.

When I have a choice, I use the *Functional Requirements Document* as described in *FIPSPUB-38*, which is a government standard on software documentation and is available from the Commerce Department. There are other methodologies, such as those described by Yourdon and Jackson, but they may be overkill at this point. The reason for this is simple: you've already verified that the logic design works by exercising the prototype. The process of producing the requirements document is primarily an expository process, describing the operation of the current machine. Much of the requirements analysis available in the other approaches is unnecessary at this point.

The Implementation Document

Once the requirements document has been completed, we can proceed to the real meat of the issue—the production of the implementation plan. This document describes the target software we intend to produce; therefore, we must read and analyze the original prototype sources to determine how we will construct the target system.

Analysis plays a major role here because we are not going to be able to copy the source from the prototyping to the target machine and make it work 10 times faster. If we could, we would just use the prototype as the final system as well. The instances will be rare, but during a career in the RP environment, you may find smaller projects where the prototype was deemed acceptable for production use.

Analysis is a major issue here and you must make special efforts to understand that this analysis consists of two distinct tasks done in an interleaved fashion. First, you have to analyze the prototype from Smalltalk's viewpoint, understanding how and why things were done the way they were. In doing this, you are most likely going to encounter sections of code where it's obvious that something better could be done. If you choose to improve things, you should stick closely to improving the quality of the algorithms themselves, and only when you are doing a port to another OOP environment.

Prototype Implementation Section

This particular section of the implementation document is much like the previous requirements, insofar as it is constructed by a reverse engineering of the existing prototype. Therefore, it is primarily an expository process. Instead of describing the surface effects of the running prototype system in order to build a requirements document, the internal logic of the system will be described to produce the implementation document that describes the prototype software.

Now that we are in possession of a functional requirements specification and an implementation document, we could pretend that we had developed the prototype by analyzing the requirements, producing the implementation specification, and writing the prototype in one pass. What is important to note here is that the conventional design methodologies concentrate too much on the purely logical issues and thereby fail to recognize that software development is non-deterministic. Modern software development requires that you use exploratory techniques where you interact extensively with clients to determine the requirements for their systems. Rapid prototyping recognizes this by allowing you to separate the development process into two distinct steps. The first step, which has been the primary focus of this book, involves the process of working with a client and a rapid prototyping platform such as Smalltalk. It is inherently fuzzy and unsuited to extensive use of formal analysis techniques. Communication skills are worth as much as logical skills in such an environment. Once this step has been completed, as it is now, the deliverables from the prototyping effort are exactly what we need to satisfy the formal analysis requirements. As I've shown, the first step is to work backward to these documents from the running prototype software.

Target Platform Contrasts

The next step is to describe the target platform, in terms of the tools you will be using to implement the software and the environment the software will run in. Your goal is to ensure that when you begin the actual writing of the implementation plan, you have the similarities and differences fixed firmly in your mind. I call this set of data the *delta document* between two platforms; it represents what is different between them. In writing the target platform implementation plan, your job is to translate the prototype specification into the target specification. This delta document indicates what sections of the prototype implementation you will need to examine.

The delta document needs to be organized so it is of use from the prototype's or the final system's point of view and it serves as the gateway between the prototype implementation and the target implementation. This document is the filter that the prototype implementation passes through in order to become a target implementation.

Although the description of this section is short and straightforward, the document we are describing is not small. If you are using a Macintosh running C as the target environment, this document consists of, among other things:

- The complete set of Macintosh documentation.
- Documents on third-party OOP interface libraries or a detailed document on conversion from objects and messages to functions and procedural control.
- All the project documentation.
- Documentation on all external systems we will be using.
- Standard library of algorithms, design, and language books.

You can see that, although I call this a translation process, it is decidedly non-trivial. None of the above references will actually tell us what to do, they will simply tell us the rules that will constrain our selections.

You should not try to actually determine the how and whys behind using all of this data in developing the target implementation plan. The only task at this time is to collect together all the relevant information so it can be used in the next section.

Target Implementation Section

The final section in the implementation document has the distinction of being the one requiring the most work, producing the most stress, and generally being a problem child. This is the document where you "translate" the prototype implementation specification into the target system's terms, supposedly switching one operating paradigm for another. This is true to a certain degree.

As I've been saying, the standard methodologies depend on clearly defined problems that don't have loose threads and vague ideas. Today, this requirement directly conflicts with the modern software development environment, and is causing us problems. We can remove the source of this conflict by having a very formal specification of our task.

To produce the target implementation document, we are attempting to produce a document that means exactly the same thing as the prototype implementation document, except in terms of the target machine and environment. While I do not deny this is a complex task, I do believe it is a logical task, with clearly defined parameters. For this reason, it is an excellent set of data to use with traditional design methodologies.

With the prototype implementation and delta sections, you have all the necessary information to satisfy these methodologies. Given that you have correctly reverse engineered the prototype to produce its implementation document, you are guaranteed that the specifications are both correct and complete, because they are based on the prototype accepted by the client. On the other hand, this is also a good reason not to deviate from the prototype when you don't like the way it does things, for you lose this guarantee of correctness and completeness.

Because you have information of this caliber, you can whip out your favorite standard design methodology, draw your ERDs, DFDs, flowcharts, waterfalls, and anything else you use in your standard development. You will find that whatever your tools, you will be able to complete the process in much less time—the prototyping session has removed all the ambiguities in the specification.

OOPS Implementation

When the process of writing these documents has been completed, we have a traditional task ahead of us: implementing and testing each of the items scheduled for implementation. As I am not discussing traditional implementation scenarios, I will stop at this point and discuss another related issue for this chapter. (Suffice it to say that there are hundreds of books out there that take you through formal design and implementation environments and what you have from the prototyping process will serve you well in any of them.)

I would like to concentrate on issues involving ports between OOP environments and non-OOP environments. As you first saw in Chapter 11, there are only a few specific reasons I would willingly port to a non-OOP environment:

- My choice of an implementation language is tightly constrained.
- I am never going to change the prototype again.
- The final implementation is going to be an exact copy of the prototype, functionally speaking.
- I have very serious space or speed considerations.

The best option by far is to use a recognized OOPL system such as C++, Objective-C, Think C, Eiffel, or a similar system. In such a case, you are simply translating from one OOP paradigm to another, making these the easiest of the ports. One point you should consider is whether or not you need the system to support loose typing, which means the system must implement dynamic message dispatching.

If you are using any polymorphic functions in your prototype, you either have to use a system such as Objective-C or Think C (a language that provides dynamic dispatch facilities). These languages provide a mechanism to select a specific function based on the class of the object which the function is being applied to. For example, if I implemented the message *m* in the three classes Class1, Class2, and

Class3, and I wanted to send *m* to an object O declared as an instance of class Object, a statically linked system such as C++ would call the function *m* assigned to the specific class we had typed as O. In short, it would use whatever it knew at compile time, assuming the runtime environment wouldn't do anything like change its mind. C++ provides a virtual keyword, which bypasses these problems, but the language itself is not oriented towards dynamically dispatched systems.

In the previous example, a dynamically linked system keeps a table for every kind of object in the system, a table which defines the functions that class implements. A dynamic system can get an object to identify its own class, use this information to identify the method table, and then use the method name to index to the appropriate function in the table.

A prototype using loose typing or polymorphic method organizations requires that you either port the design to a target environment which supports these requirements or remove this behavior from the prototype. Removing these behaviors is time consuming and has certain negative impacts on maintenance and enhancements because you are replacing a very sophisticated logical construct with one that may be faster and is definitely more primitive. At times this is a necessary evil and you have to go through all of the prototype to ensure that:

- All classes segregate the data they store by class. If a class put objects of class C1, C2, and C3 into a List L, it should be modified to separate them into three lists, LC1, LC2, and LC3.
- All polymorphic function names have the name of their class prefixed. This means that the print method in the class Freight would become FreightPrint.
- Verify that all existing variable casting is not depending on the ability of an object to identify itself. View casts from general classes to more specific classes with skepticism.

These three steps will ensure that the system no longer contains heterogeneous lists or polymorphic function definitions. When this is true, you have maintenance problems, such as a large number of ex-polymorphic functions with individual and ridiculously long names. However, this code will execute more efficiently.

If you must use a non-OO language, then you might consider one of the utility libraries that can be used to extend C, Pascal, and other languages so that they support the OO paradigm. I personally recommend one package, the Objects in C (OIC) package written by John Wainwright. It implements a dynamic message dispatching model based on the CLOS design. I've used this software with great success on the MAC; it's available as shareware, in source form, on most public data networks. I strongly suggest you examine this material if you are working in a straight C environment.

If you have absolutely no choice but to convert to another language that does not support objects, you should not attempt any kind of line-by-line translation of the code. Instead, you should attempt to understand the function of each of the methods and to first work on re-expressing them in efficient terms in the new language. Following this, if the language supports structures and functions, you can link all of your translated objects together by putting the object's instance variables into the structure and passing this structure as the first parameter to each of the reimplemented method functions. For example, if the method *m* has been implemented in class *C*, and we had defined a structure *S* that mapped to *C*'s instance variables, all of the new calls could be written in the following form:

```
Cm(&S,{trailing parameters});
```

In short, object-oriented techniques are good for both implementation and maintenance reasons and in cases where the code is being ported to a non-OOP environment, certain steps can be taken to minimize the damage to the OOP model. In any case, the model is expendable after the implementation section has been written, the only issue involved is whether we can reuse some of the platform-specific design.

Summary

In this chapter I have tried to show the bridge from the RP environment to the more traditional software development environment. Now that the prototype is finished and we are preparing to move the software to the final platform, we have dealt with all of the soft issues and can successfully use the harder design methodologies.

As I stated previously, I am not an anarchist and I am not arguing that traditional design techniques be broken. My point is that they require a large collection of hard facts in order to be successfully used; hard facts that aren't always available to the system's developer when he or she begins to design a new software package.

By using the RP approach, we can work with the client to extract these requirements, using the operating prototype to check our assumptions, ensuring that we and our clients share the same vision. When the prototype has been completed, it provides us with the detail necessary to satisfy traditional design requirements. In short, RP admits that formal specifications cannot be plucked from thin air for a complex software system, rather they must be identified through an exploratory process. If the product of this process is an operating prototype, then we can apply more logical tools to the task of reverse engineering the prototype, thereby producing the information necessary to implement the real system on the target platform.

In conclusion, that's really all there is to it. Not that there aren't a myriad of details involved in the process, but the central premise is that you use a flexible, powerful OO language with a rich class library in order to do exploratory programming. From this will come your prototype, which is computer software and therefore, should be logical. Given that you have worked with the client throughout this process and they have accepted the prototype, you have good odds that you can satisfy the requirements of the formal design mechanisms on the first pass and create the software on the target machine with a minimum of fuss.

- Make sure the client *signs off* on the prototype.
- Make sure the client knows future change requests won't be accepted as willingly as during the prototyping process.
- Reverse engineer the Functional Requirements Document (FRD) from the working prototype.
- Reverse engineer the implementation plan based on the implementation of the prototype, but remember to take target platform issues into account.

CHAPTER 13

Porting Object Engines

Skill in manipulating symbols is a talent, not evidence of divine guidance.

In this final "working" chapter of the book, I am going to discuss new issues about object-oriented software, primarily by drawing out the similarities between the behavior of objects in an OOP system and the behavior of things in the real world. This discussion will show you how you can use your general experience to help with designing and implementing object-oriented systems.

I will first address a specific entity that can be found in many OO programs. This entity is an *object engine*, which is a complex runtime entity constructed from a set of cooperating objects. Object engines are essentially higher-order dynamic classes, meaning that they come in to being when the program initializes itself, and disappear when the program terminates. Engines are of great value in OOP design because they, like normal classes, can be ported from one application to another with a minimum of fuss and they can represent more complex entities than simple classes. Classes describe how static objects operate, engines describe how dynamic runtime systems operate.

Following the discussion of object engines, you will see how to apply various concepts from the real world to object-oriented systems. Specifically, I will deal with how biological models can be applied to OO systems in order to define their behavior in terms compatible with the system itself.

Object Engines

Consider the task we were confronted with a few chapters back, when we needed to establish a connection between the external database and the freight management system. In doing this, I pointed out we had two masters to serve in that we needed to satisfy the requirements of the remote database and our application. Although I didn't detail the code at this point, there would have been two distinct sections of code, one dealing with using the remote database and one dealing with the local application.

This would be true regardless of the type of design methodology used because you should always divide a problem into small, related components. This is why many OO programmers, after learning the paradigm, realize this is the way they've been trying to do things all along. The OOP system simply provides them with an environment that helps them achieve their objective.

At runtime, these two sets of classes (the remote database and the local application) are used to create a set of objects, where each object is tied in some way to objects of other classes in these sets. Operating together, these objects manifest a behavior, that allows the rest of the system to deal with all of them in terms of some unified whole. In other words, the system deals with all objects as a single complex object and ignores their individual characteristics. The design is actually dealing with an abstraction that encompasses all the distinct objects— an abstraction that exists at runtime, but not at compile time.

This behavior, when naturally exhibited by elements of the system, is an indicator of what I call an object engine. An object engine is a group of task-related objects that, when hooked together at runtime, perform some identifiable function. Object engines must define a task where the surface interface to the task is less complex than the internal operation of a task.

Consider the average car engine as an example. You can take the engine out of the car by disconnecting the electrical, drive, and fuel systems. The interface between these systems and the engine is fairly straightforward and less complex than the internal operation of the engine itself. The engine can be dealt with as an engine, as opposed to a collection of crankshafts and pistons and oil pumps. In our system, we deal with the DBMS interface, rather than with all of the individual classes that work together to make this a reality.

Classes are designed to implement things that exist in the real world or concepts that are compatible with the way the real world operates. Classes represent things and their methods represent capabilities of these things. This is quite similar to the way we describe and categorize everything we encounter in our lives. It isn't surprising that we find constructs in our systems that share certain desirable characteristics with their real-world counterparts.

In this example I have picked a more complex engine, one that has multiple classes and multiple interfaces. This behavior is not necessarily confined to multiple classes working together—there can be only a single class working as an engine. In such cases you will find that only a few of the available messages are used for external communication and that most are used for internal communication. You will also find that a fairly simple looking input message to the system can make the system go through long and complex internal operations before producing an equally simplistic result.

In short, you can identify engines within your code by locating those objects that, by themselves or with others, perform complex operations based on simple input. These are engines which can be detached from the system and used in the future. They represent a more complex concept than the simple class and they provide the runtime system a regular, simple interface to a complex task. In cases where an engine is constructed from a single class, you won't be able to find much difference between the engine's runtime behavior and its apparent behavior just by reading the software. Complex engines, those using 10 or more instances of other complex classes in concert, have a behavior that can't be easily ascertained from examination of their constituent class code. This is not an impossible task, but it does require that you go through the dynamic runtime relationships between all the linked objects and determine what internal operations take place under what conditions. To debug such an engine is easy, you simply follow the flow of control through the system until it encounters the nasty bit. Completely defining the behavior of such a system is difficult because the entire system was built from small pieces that were bolted together in the running system. Although we created this for the system's use, it is only the system that actually brings the objects together into a single functioning unit.

A while ago, I read an observation that said if you were to take all the designers of a new microprocessor and lock them in a room together until they could tell you the function of every gate in the chip, they'd never get out. The system is simply too complex to understand as a whole; it must be built in pieces that are hooked together by an agreed upon set of rules.

Reusing Engines

Once you find an engine, what you do with it depends on what kind of engine you have found and whether you are considering the reuse or porting of criteria. Porting criteria applies to all engines, but it is first necessary for you to understand a little of the engine's anatomy. We will therefore focus first on that anatomy so we can determine what issues will affect the port and whether the engine can be reused in future projects.

The first step in examining an engine is to examine its points of contact with the external system. Every engine has three primary points of contact with the external system. The first two connect the engine to the system so it can receive inputs from the system and send outputs to it. The final point is broader and can be defined as the environment in which the engine expects to operate.

The two easiest classes of external interfaces are those where the interface is identifiable as a purely application-oriented interface or as a purely system-oriented interface. The first kind is easily recognized and deals with concepts of interest only to this application. For example, we might find that the code we implemented to print waybills on preprinted forms formed an engine, where the inputs were the raw waybill data and the outputs were raw printer data, and where a lot of confusion occurred in the middle, during the process of moving from one form to another. Although this is an engine, we can't expect to reuse it as an engine, although we might well reuse some of its classes. On the other hand, the interface to the auditing system expects records from us in a standard form and it only returns to us with a permission granted or denied message. We could reuse this in another application for Schroeder Trucking since we have an engine that deals with the interface to the auditing system in terms of the auditing system, as opposed to the terms of the freight management software.

Our DBMS example is unfortunately a member of the third class of external interface, where one side is application specific and the other side is reusable. In our case, the DBMS engine interfaces with the external database, which is a capability we would like to reuse. It also interfaces with the freight management application, a capability we don't want to reuse.

Engines are usually created to deal with more complex software management tasks. These engines must be decomposed to separate them into their respective elements, if possible. What you are trying to find is whether or not these engines naturally divide into two distinct engines, one dealing with the database side of things and the other dealing with the application.

Most complex engines can be easily broken in two. The reason for this is simple, if the designer has followed the principles of modular design up to now, it is unlikely that he or she will abandon them inside an engine. If, on the other hand, they have willfully ignored these principles, it's probably an accident that they have constructed an engine at all.

To determine how to separate an engine into its parts, you need to make two sets to hold all of the classes in the original engine. Into one of these sets you will place those classes that deal with application requirements and into the other you will place those classes that deal with external system requirements. Having done this, you may find you have exhausted the set of classes in the original engine or you may find that you have a few left over. If you have a few left over and you cannot justify calling them either application specific or system generic, then try to see if they might be used as an interface between the application and system components of the engine. In very complex engines, such as those that interact with external databases, you may find they contain several classes whose function is to help the engine navigate the application/system barrier. In an engine, these are essentially *transport* classes, as they transport data and commands through this barrier.

In any case, your next step is to determine the messages that cross the application/system barrier, either from one side to the other or by using an intervening transport class.

In identifying the messages, you should be sensitive to many of the same issues as you were in identifying the engine itself. The actual barrier is a very complex entity. The function of the methods and possibly the classes that navigate this barrier is to encapsulate this complexity so that each side can deal with the issue in simpler terms.

After you have identified this barrier and the mechanisms through which data and commands are transported to it, you can define the original engine as the product of two interlocking engines. The first of these, the external database interface, is one that you will set up for future reuse, whereas the application side will not.

Porting Engines

Unlike reuse, porting considerations apply equally to all engines, regardless of whether they are strictly tied to the current application or are of general use throughout the system. When porting any engine, you should remember that there are certain characteristics that make it an engine and you should exploit these characteristics in the porting process. Surprisingly, these basics also apply to ports to object-oriented environments and to non-object-oriented environments.

Foremost in the similarities between object-oriented ports and non-object-oriented ports is the fact that any engine has a well-defined organizational structure and a well-defined control structure. Furthermore, these structures are geared towards the tasks performed by the engine, as opposed to being geared towards characteristics of the porting platform itself.

For this reason alone, you should port engines between platforms with as few structural changes as possible. Even if you port to a non-OO environment, you should preserve the modular structure of the engine, in terms of the logical units that compose it and the commands it responds to. To accomplish this you must continue with the decomposition of the engine, identifying each of the separate objects it contains and replicating them as closely as possible in the target environment.

The immutability of engine structures during the porting process is a critical issue, especially since many events will try to prevent you from doing this. You must monitor this process closely and ensure that, while the target platform may force you to diverge in spots, the overall structure is maintained faithfully. If you do not succeed in this, you will no longer have an engine; instead, you'll have a loose collection of code that may not behave in the ways you desire. Engines are elements of software that evolve naturally from the requirements and internal structure of the system. To change them is to guarantee that they will no longer be engines and will no longer be in sync with the program's requirements or its internal structure.

When changes must be made, this is a difficult process when porting to the non-OOP environment. As I stated previously, the porting of an engine is a process that is the same, regardless of the target platform. What I didn't say was that in porting to a non-OOP environment you are expected to go through whatever efforts are necessary to ensure this is the case.

The first issue is the decomposition of the engine into objects, or modules. It is very important that you not decide this is the time to restructure the logic within the engine. You can wander through the engine's code and note little things you could do here and there to make it more efficient—within reason this isn't a bad idea. You must not, however, do anything that seriously modifies the operating characteristics of the engine. This would be a bad idea because you would be deviating from the specification manifested by the prototype software and, additionally, engines are complex, interlocked entities that are usually rendered non-operational by such efforts. The evolution of an engine is a reasonably natural process in software development of this type, and this evolution tends to follow the path of least resistance. If you've successfully identified an engine, do your best to leave it alone.

In porting an engine to a new non-OOP environment, you want to create modules that are structured like the classes that compose the prototype engine. All of the messages will be translated to function or subroutine calls and it is important that you distinguish between those that are reserved for use within the engine itself and those that are used by external users of the engine. Those internal messages should be restricted to use within the engine modules themselves. This is done by declaring them as local or static functions. The external calls are what you will make available to outside users so they can operate the engine successfully.

Engine Environments

The final issue in dealing with engines is the definition of their operating environment. In the OOP platform this environment can be defined as the set of classes used internally by the engine to accomplish its task. In the case of our database engine, this would include such things as Collections to manage the database data and SerialPorts or Sockets to handle communications with the physical database application. When considering the possible reuse of an engine in the future, or the porting of an engine to a new host platform, it is vitally important that you have a list of all these classes and a plan for dealing with their requirements.

You will have to satisfy the requirements indicated by these classes before the engine will operate in a new system. In doing this, there are two possible paths you can follow. You can embed the capabilities directly within the engine itself or you can reimplement the class in the new system.

If you choose to embed the code directly within the engine you want to be careful that you select only those points where this is truly the correct thing to do. When you are confronted by an engine that uses a single class in one location, and this class isn't used anywhere else in the prototype, you may wish to integrate the functions of this class into the engine. What you are doing is taking an existing system class and treating it as if it were a component of the engine itself.

While this approach is efficient from both an implementation and an operational viewpoint, you must be certain it will not backfire on you. If you later find you need to implement the class anyway to solve some other requirement, you will have been forced to do the same work twice. To add insult to injury, you will also be forced to go back to the engine, remove the code you have installed, and make the engine use the newly installed class.

If you decide to embed external class logic directly within the engine, you should consider the future carefully. The bottom line is that you should implement this logic directly within the engine if, and only if, you use it in one place and you never expect it to exist as a stand-alone class in the future.

Most of the environmental requirements of the engine will be implemented as separate, stand-alone classes. This is primarily due to the fact that much of the engines environmental requirements will overlap with the general system requirements. It is highly likely that our database engine will use instances of the Collection class to hold its internal data. It is also likely that the database engine is not the only user of this class, so we're already operating under the assumption that the Collection class will be implemented as a stand-alone unit.

In porting an engine, as in porting any of the code, the implementation document will be the most valuable guide. If this document has been done properly, it will have accurately determined the requirements of the system and the dependencies between the various elements you will be implementing. In the case of classes that should be moved into the engine itself, you will find that only the engine is dependant on these classes. As for the rest, you will usually find a rat's nest of dependencies, especially when common classes such as Collection and its subtypes are used.

General Biological Models

Object-oriented software design and development shares a great deal with accepted biological models. Many sources on object-oriented programming describe the environment as an evolutionary one, where programs grow in complexity and capacity over time, as opposed to the traditional environments where programs are created in a few passes. The growth of the class hierarchy itself can be seen as the growth of genetic material, much of which can be used in the formation of future programs. The distinction between the object and the messages that move between them can be viewed in much the same light as the organs of the body and the nervous system that connects the organs.

The job of an OO programmer is to stand with one foot in this paradigm and the other in a traditional design paradigm. I do not agree with those that argue that OOP calls for us to divorce ourselves totally from the older design methodologies, for those methodologies address reliability and maintenance issues that the traditional OOP environment ignores. Conversely, one cannot depend only on these standard methodologies for the simple reason that they do not operate well in the rapid prototyping environment, which we have seen is necessary to successfully navigate the murky waters of modern software design projects.

To successfully meld these two approaches, the OOP designer must deal with each of these aspects in its own terms. The OOP model can be accurately described in primarily biological terms, whereas the traditional design methods are defined in a reductionist manner. In dealing with the closure of prototyping and the beginning of the porting process, it is time for the designer to move from the biological model to the reductionist model. This isn't hard, assuming that the designer keeps the two sides separated and does not succumb to temptation to redefine the OOP prototype in reductionist terms.

When you develop the implementation document for the final porting operation you will have to read through the code of the prototype and reduce it to produce the implementation document, which describes how to reimplement it without undue sensitivity to the original development environment. This is unquestionably a process of reduction, but if you examine the situation closely you will find that the process is confined to the decomposition of the logical instructions that compose the program. Nowhere does this document directly address the interaction, between these objects, that creates the running program.

This is a subtle and important difference and it lies at the heart of recognizing the biological nature of OO programs. The biological description of a program, or a particular element of a program, is not a blow-by-blow description of the logic of the code. Instead, the biological model describes (in terms of their function as opposed to their internal mechanics), the dynamic relationships between the various objects as they run on the host system.

This is the most difficult part of OO design and programming, the delicate balance between the reductionistic view of the static code that composes the software, and the holistic view that describes the operation of the running system. In many cases you will find that these two descriptions appear to form disjointed sets, where it is difficult to define why the code produces the effects it does. What you must remember is that the success of the object-oriented coding paradigm is that it allows the software constructs to naturally reflect the behavior of the system they are implementing.

Many traditional languages such as C and Pascal have a strong procedural bias that dominates the structure and dynamic behavior of the running system. In short, this emphasis on structure is so strong in the language that it inevitably biases everything implemented within the language. The cleavage between objects and messages in an OOP system allows us to easily separate the internal logic of code segments from the stimuli that control these segments. For this reason, the internal code is, like all computer software, procedurally oriented and lives within a purely reductionist framework. But the messages themselves are less bound to such a tight view of the world. Although they unquestionably do arise from the procedural flow of the running system, they aren't as tightly coupled to its internal logic. Instead, their logical basis is on the system's overall behavior and not on its constituent parts.

For those of you who may doubt me, there is a simple test you can perform that may reassure you. I assume you are familiar with the standard concept of control and data flow documentation and how this documentation is generated from traditional programs. Take what you have designed for the freight management system, on paper or in your head, and produce a data flow and control flow document from it. You should discover fairly quickly that a message-based architecture is not as amenable to this kind of analysis as is the more traditional procedure calling architecture. You can generate such documents, but the control flow is often far more complex and variable, and is not extracted by simply scanning the code for the various subroutine calls.

When examining OO programs in detail, you must therefore divide your examination into two parts. To understand how the code itself operates, depend on the traditional analysis skills you have used up to now. Regardless of the actual language, these are logical instructions running on a computer, therefore the standard techniques work well here. But when it comes to understanding the behavior of larger units within the system, especially when concentrating on runtime effects, you aren't really concerned with what the various code modules do. Instead, you focus on the messages that flow between these various modules and what happens within the system as these messages pass through it. In doing this, you want to identify the system's "natural" internal model, which often has an underlying biological concept. In short, decompose code into its parts, but compose system operations into a whole that efficiently defines all activities of the system without resorting to exhaustive techniques.

Summary

In conclusion, I will stress that this is not a book on new age programming and I am most definitely not ascribing metaphysical aspects to program development. What I am saying is that much of the power of OOP prototyping and design is that it allows you to construct systems that are based on two cooperating models. The first, and more traditional, is the reductionist model that describes the behavior of individual methods in individual classes. The second is the holistic model that defines the runtime behavior of the system and its components. Although both are rooted in the system's code, the fact that these two models coexist as distinct entities is one of the key concepts in OO systems.

To offer an example I heard at a conference on neural networks, if you put a bunch of gas molecules in a box, you can describe their behavior based on the standard physical laws that govern the behavior of gas molecules, in terms of their bouncing off each other, resulting pressures, and so on. Put a whole bunch of gas molecules in a box and they can carry sound waves, which isn't something addressed by any of the laws governing the behavior of individual gas molecules. The central point is that once any system, physical or logical, passes a certain point of complexity, there is an exponential increase in its capabilities due to the increased amount of interaction between its components.

CHAPTER 14

Rapid Prototyping Review

Things always get worse before they get better.
Who ever said things would get better?

In this book I have shown the rapid prototyping process, from the initial decision that something ought to be done to make things better through the determination of exactly what would make things better, and the final realization of this concept in a piece of prototype software. I have shown that this is as much a soft issue involving the desires of the client community as it is a hard issue dealing with the rigors of software design.

As you have seen, this process is somewhat unstructured, insofar as you cannot expect to begin operating within a clearly defined framework. You are no doubt aware of the fact that software development itself is a highly structured activity. The central issue in rapid prototyping is the mesh of these two requirements, the realization that success will only come when both requirements are satisfied, the understanding that declaring one or the other of these requirements invalid is a simply a prescription for failure.

To succeed, you must follow the steps I have illustrated in this book. I don't mean you should slavishly follow each little detail, rather that you stay true to the big picture. Your task in prototyping new software is to work with the clients and the computer, so that all entities involved are moving forward together in refining the definition of the problem, therein producing a solution for the problem.

Review

One of the central issues in rapid prototyping is flexibility, in both the designer's approach and the capabilities of the development system. You cannot proceed assuming that anything is written in stone, therefore you always need to be roughly estimating the stability of each of the tasks you are performing. Some things, such as the core architecture of the system, manifested in its overall "look and feel" are laid down fairly early and don't change too much through the development cycle. The individual components of the system, such as individual user interfaces, the behavior of specific internal sections, and so on can change more often and are often in flux right up to the time the prototype is finally completed.

Your job as a rapid prototyper is to work with the client to extract specifications for their new software through an *exploratory* process that we call rapid prototyping. In doing this, you must work from general issues such as what the software is supposed to do into the more specific issues of exactly how it will accomplish these tasks. This is related to, but not identical to, the top-down design methodologies you may have already studied. It is useful to apply your experience in top-down design to solving these problems, but it is also important that you know this is a new approach, and you cannot blindly apply the precepts of top-down design to the problem.

The first thing you must do is to work with the client to move beyond the recognition that there is a problem to an agreed upon mechanism for solving the problem. As this forms much of the overall "flavor" of the system you will be producing, it is important that you get this right. There are certain things you can use to your advantage.

The primary characteristic you can exploit is that you are dealing with a conceptual issue. Although this issue will have wide-ranging impacts on the prototype and the final system, it is somewhat soft, meaning that you do not have to rigorously define exactly what you want to do. Instead, by exploiting the fact that you are dealing with the "concept" of the software here, you can use anecdotal descriptions to define to the client what you intend on doing, much as I illustrated in the first two chapters. Your objective is not to lay down a complete plan of how this software is to be implemented, in fact you are not even interested in implementation details. Your concern at this point is simply on defining *why* this software is being written in the first place, which will tell you *what* is expected of it.

After having reached an agreement with the client on what the objective of the software is to be, you can begin to concentrate on how this objective will be reached. This is best done in anecdotal terms, which means that even with the objective formulated, you still do not have enough information in hand to simply code up a solution. Much work will be required with the client personnel to determine how things are done now and what needs to be done in the future to reach this objective. Additionally, while the end objective itself has been defined, its detailed characteristics are still unknown.

For this reason, you will want to first concentrate on a mock-up of the user interface, so that you and the clients have something you can interact with, a skeleton you can slowly flesh out as you reach a deeper understanding of the problem and its solution. You cannot code this interface in a vacuum however, so you will need to develop the interface in parallel with the central objects within the system. To do so, start with *views* of these objects, for the simple reason that it is often easier to understand things by drawing a picture of them as opposed to wading through reams of text describing them.

When you have defined the basic characteristics of the central objects and the views that can be used to examine and alter them, it is time to begin working closely with the clients. You will need to start operating the prototype, so that the clients can sit down with it and form their opinions about what should be done next by interacting with what has been done up to now. At first, as the software is still more of an idea than a reality, you will find it necessary to "dummy up" the software, hard wiring in the data displays. This is due to the fact that the final system will be actually capable of retrieving this data from some external source, but the current system isn't too sure about such things. Therefore, you initially hardwire data into the system so that the views come up and look like they are doing something intelligent, even if they really aren't.

With the operating prototype in hand, you begin working more closely with the client, meeting with them often to extract detailed information to guide your progress through the development maze. Slowly you will begin replacing the hardwired data and connections between elements of the interface with mechanisms to actually manage this data and to support real "navigation" through the elements of the interface. This process will continue right up to the time the prototype is deemed complete, the only thing being that as time passes and the major issues are dealt with, you find yourself spending a fair amount of time on what appear to be minor cosmetic issues. These cosmetic issues are not as trivial as they seem, for if they are satisfied there is a large likelihood the end users will actually enjoy using the software and be productive with it, whereas if they are ignored, the end users may in turn ignore the software. Such a result is exactly what rapid prototyping is meant to prevent.

As you progress in the development of the prototype and the interface elements begin to stabilize, you can concentrate on developing some of the internal algorithms, especially those that deal with interfacing to external systems. In rapid prototyping you often will not be spending a great deal of time prototyping internal algorithms, for the simple reason that most internal algorithms are quite sensitive to the specific language they are developed in. If, for example, your final target language, C, and the target machine include a sophisticated math co-processor, it's an exercise in futility to prototype trigonometric functions—this effort is unnecessary in the final system. What does stay constant, regardless of the final target language or system, is that all interfaces will have to be prototyped. Where many existing prototyping tools fall short is in the assumption that interfaces are simply screen displays the user interacts with. Interfaces also include connections to external systems and connections between components of the system being developed. Both of these areas are as deserving of your attention during the prototyping phase as are the pure user interfaces.

Finally, you will reach a point where you and the client agree that the prototype is complete and reflects exactly what is expected of the final software package. Assuming that you have always kept in mind the requirements and capabilities of the target system, both hardware and software, you should be confronted with a fairly straightforward reverse engineering process where you use the prototype software as the blueprint for developing the specifications for the final software. This is the gateway between the fuzzy world of exploratory software development and the formal world of rigid systems analysis.

This is one of the more subtle but important contributions of the RP process. By allowing software development to be fuzzy through the initial design process and then providing a clear mechanism for bridging the gap to formal system development tools, RP allows us to bring new tools to bear on new problems. At the same time, it allows us to continue using those tools that have served us well over the years *in a form compatible with their basic requirements.*

In conclusion, the rapid prototyping process involves:

1. Identification of the strategic goal to be solved in anecdotal terms
2. Definition of the core elements (objects) within the system and the user interface linked to these views.
3. Iterative enhancement of the views and core components of the system until they possess the desired level of functionality.
4. Development of the interfaces between internal elements of the system and external systems.

5. Production of a final implementation plan and detailed requirements analysis based on the finished prototype.
6. Production of the final release system.

Prototyping Platform Issues

I would like to stress what is important in the prototype by offering another option for using the Smalltalk language in the rapid prototyping environment. By doing this I hope to illustrate exactly what the key issues are in any rapid prototyping platform, so that you can use what I have presented in this book across a variety of platforms, assuming they meet certain basic requirements.

For many years I have used the Smalltalk language as a prototyping vehicle and have been quite satisfied with its performance. Given recent developments in languages and platforms I have begun to use another language to perform some of my prototyping, because it provides me with most of the advantages of Smalltalk while at the same time it is less "distant" from my final target language, C.

The system I have started to use is the Symantec Think C 4.0 package, which is available for the Apple Macintosh computer. Think C implements a subset of the C++ language, sometimes called C+. Others have called this language "Object Pascal in C."

Object-oriented programming techniques are vital in the RP process, for the many reasons I have given throughout this book. But object-oriented programming alone does not make a rapid prototyping environment. In addition to the basic object-oriented capabilities of the development language, a robust class hierarchy is required to provide you with most of the essential classes required for software development. Think C provides this in the *Think Class Library* (TCL), which is an excellent class library written by Greg Dow for Symantec. TCL falls halfway between a minimal class library such as those found in several public domain packages (such as John Wainwright's OIC) and a full-featured class library (the Smalltalk-80 system from ParcPlace).

Even still, an object-oriented language and a class library alone are not enough to form a good rapid prototyping environment. Apple Computer makes a rather large and sophisticated class library called *MacApp* which can be used with either C++ or Object Pascal, but neither of these environments is truly suited to the RP process. There is one more vital requirement that must be satisfied in order for a "language system" to be suitable for rapid prototyping.

I stated early that much of the software in an RP project is a moving target, constantly being modified and changed based on your interactions with clients. Change is one of the main constants in the RP process, and to survive in this environment you must be able to handle changes rapidly, without having the entire thing come apart.

Smalltalk is the unquestioned master at this, for as you change and save each individual method within the system, the methods are automatically recompiled and the system is updated. This means that at most one method in the system will be out of date—and this is only if you have neglected to save your changes between the last edit and your attempt to run the system.

Think C is almost as good as Smalltalk, as only a single command need be invoked to completely rebuild and relink the application. Dependencies between files are automatically identified and maintained by the system, absolving the developer of the responsibility of creating and maintaining the "make" files used to construct the application. Therefore, when you change an individual class, all you need to do to bring the running version into sync with the source code is to issue a single command instructing the system to rebuild the application.

Three capabilities are required to make a specific language environment a good rapid prototyping platform:

- An object-oriented language
- A class hierarchy implementing the standard objects used in most programs
- An environment that automatically handles update and integration tasks

These capabilities form the foundation of any RP task. If they are present in a single system, the system can be used for rapid prototyping. If any one of them is missing, the system (while it might be an excellent vehicle for final software development) is crippled.

Final Thoughts

The entire object-oriented paradigm has been fairly stable for a number of years now, even though new languages such as C++ and Eiffel have appeared recently. However, with the attention of the main body of developers coming to bear on OOP, it has once again started to move forward. Old arguments about things like multiple inheritance finally look like they may be resolved and new issues, such as those dealing with collaborative applications, are coming to the forefront.

I have been an evangelist for object-oriented programming for many years now and I must admit I am pleased to see it moving forward. The truly nice thing about the OOP paradigm is that unlike many other environments, truths in OOP are not invalidated by the discovery of new truths. Your investment of time in learning how to use object-oriented techniques, learning about class hierarchies, and learning about specific techniques such as rapid prototyping is unlikely to be invalidated by future discoveries. This is primarily due to the fact that object-oriented programming is based on a model of the "natural" world, rather than the totally artificial reality constructed by a traditional procedural language.

In conclusion, I can say that your efforts in learning the fundamentals of object-oriented programming and the application of these fundamentals in techniques such as rapid prototyping will never be made obsolete by developments in computer science, at least not until these developments do away with the need for programmers entirely. It is my hope that this book has given you the information you need to successfully deal with the realities of modern software design, and to allow you to use the tools and techniques available to you to the limit of their capabilities.

Index